FOOTBALL

DRILL

BOOK

DOUG MALLORY

MASTERS PRESS

A Division of Howard W. Sams & Co.

Published by Masters Press (A Division of Howard W. Sams & Co.)
2647 Waterfront Pkwy E. Dr., Suite 300
Indianapolis, IN 46214

10 9 8 7 6 5

Library of Congress Cataloging-in-Publication Data
Mallory, Doug, 1964 —
      Spalding football drill book / Doug Mallory.
         p.   cm. -- (The Spalding sports library.)
      ISBN 0-940279-72-X
      1. Football -- Training.   2. Football -- Coaching   I. Title.
   II. Series.
   GV953.5.M35   1993   93-34346
   796.332'07--dc20   CIP

CREDITS:
Cover design and diagrams by Julie Biddle.
Text design by Leah Marckel.
Back cover photo provided by Western Kentucky University's Sports Information Department.
Front cover photo provided by Indiana University Sports Information Department.

TABLE OF CONTENTS

ACKNOWLEDGMENTS

I'd like to take this opportunity to thank the people who made this book possible.

First, I'd like to thank the staff of Masters Press, especially Tom Bast, who approached me about writing this book, and Holly Kondras, my editor.

I would also like to thank the coaches for whom I have had the opportunity to play. I was truly blessed as a player to have been around men who taught me so much about football and more importantly about life. I would like to thank Lee Ross, my junior high coach, and Chuck Schrader, my high school coach , for the many lessons they taught me. A special thanks to Bo Schembechler, Lloyd Carr, Billy Harris, Milan Vooletich, Gary Moeller, Jerry Hanlon, Mike Gittleson and the rest of the Michigan staff for giving me five of the greatest years of my life at Michigan.

Thanks also to the coaches I have had the opportunity to work with, learn from, and become close to: Jack Harbaugh, Don Yarano, Rick Denstorff, Mike Settles, Bill Edwards, Scott Keller, Mike Haywood, Eric Campbell, Darryl Drake, and Andy Moeller for sending me information and drills pertinent to this book.

To my parents, Bill and Ellie Mallory; my brothers, Mike and Curt; and my sister, Barb, I express my deepest thanks. Without my family's influence, I would not have acquired such a deep love for the game of football. Their support has been continuous throughout my career as a player and coach.

Finally, I would like to express a loving appreciation to my wife, Lisa, for her support, devotion, and patience in completing this project.

FOREWORD

Successful football coaches share, almost invariably, the same characteristics. A love and respect for the game is essential to success. Coaches won't give the time and effort if the game is not special to them. Winning coaches like to work. They will spend time studying the game and striving to improve. They believe in basic fundamentals and want the best drills and methods to teach it. Great coaches know how to motivate players and develop winning attitudes that will bring consistent improvement and performance. Last but not least, the top coaches sincerely believe in teaching young men loyalty, honesty, and integrity. That is what football can teach when coaches stress these qualities and demand them from their players. The impact football coaches have on players is unparalleled in any other sport. The coaches must not take this lightly. The opportunity to coach this game is special. We must remember this in everything we do.

Bo Schembechler
Former Head Coach, University of Michigan

FOREWORD

Like most coaches, my staff and I are continually looking for good drills. We feel it is important that a coach has a variety of drills so the players don't become bored and "just go through the motions." The drill must have a purpose to better enhance the teaching, while also challenging the player and improving his techniques. With limited practice time, it is imperative that coaches choose drills that will most effectively teach the desired skills.

All coaches - at every level of coaching - need drill books. This drill book would immensely benefit the beginning coach as well as established coaches at the high school and college level. We all need comprehensive drill books to add to our "Coaching Libraries."

Bill Mallory
Head Coach, Indiana University

INJURY PREVENTION GUIDELINES FOR FOOTBALL

Bill Edwards, M.A., A.T.C.

Participation Physical Exam

Before participating on a sports team of any kind, athletes should complete a thorough medical history questionnaire as part of their physical examination process. This history should include information regarding family cardiac history. A good medical history is a vital part of the pre-participation examination. Student athletes who have sustained previous injury should be evaluated for rehabilitation needs prior to participation.

Preseason Conditioning

Athletes should engage in training and conditioning activities to aid in the prevention of injury. They should work at sport specific drills to condition the muscles they will need in practice. Preseason conditioning also should be done in hot weather on a gradual basis to acclimate them for the hot weather practices ahead.

Education

Athletes must be informed of the assumption of risk involved in their participation in the sport. They should be instructed in proper blocking and tackling techniques in order to prevent serious neck injuries. It must be stressed to them that hitting with the top of the head must be eliminated. The athletes must be informed of what they can do to prevent heat illness. They should be instructed in the proper care and maintenance of their protective equipment.

If you have a team doctor, he should lecture on health and injury prevention topics the first day of practice. If your team does not, see if you can find a specialist in sports medicine to come speak to your players. Most doctors will be happy to help you prepare for a safe and, hopefully, injury-free season.

A very important lesson must be taught on what to do for a non-moving player if injured. It is vital that a non-moving athlete not be moved by teammates or opponents. Coaches should stress this point at every practice, until players can repeat it in their sleep. Paralysis may occur by improper movement of a neck injury. An athletics trainer or coach should be summoned immediately.

Emergency Care

A comprehensive emergency plan must be in place including personal, equipment, supplies, and an action plan. Everyone involved should be fully prepared to put the plan into action. Remember that players with head or neck injuries are not to return to play without a physician's approval.

Environmental Concerns

The facilities being used should constantly be evaluated and inspected for potential hazards.

During hot weather, heat illness prevention is a must. The following is a list of preventative measures to take in dealing with the heat:

1. Gradually acclimating the players to conditioning in the heat.

2. Unlimited cold water available at all times. Encourage pre-practice fluid intake to assure hydration before starting and continue fluids during and after practice. Provide rest periods during practice to aid in fluid absorption.

3. Choose uniforms that allow for optimum cooling. During hot weather, helmets and pads should be removed when not needed.

4. Schedule practices at the cooler times of the day and monitor the heat by using a sling psychrometer to measure temperature and humidity. Use a recommended chart that gives practice recommendations based on the readings.

5. Be watchful for athletes with signs and symptoms of heat illness and treat them quickly and appropriately.

6. Identify susceptible athletes:

   - Large athletes.
   - Overweight athletes.
   - Those with previous heat illness.
   - Those who are ill.
   - Those with high percentages of weight loss (3% or higher) during practices (this should be monitored by use of weight charts used before and after each practice).

Uniforms and Equipment

Equipment must be properly fitted. The primary guideline should be to follow the manufacturer's guidelines with regard to fitting, maintenance and reconditioning. An inventory of helmets should be kept with dates of manufacture, purchase, and reconditioning.

FOOTBALL

DRILL

BOOK

Key to Diagrams

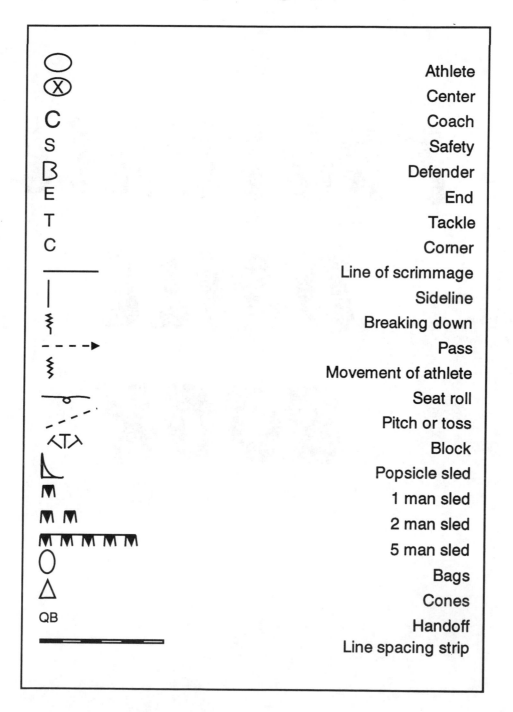

Symbol	Meaning
	Athlete
	Center
C	Coach
S	Safety
	Defender
E	End
T	Tackle
C	Corner
	Line of scrimmage
	Sideline
	Breaking down
	Pass
	Movement of athlete
	Seat roll
	Pitch or toss
	Block
	Popsicle sled
	1 man sled
	2 man sled
	5 man sled
	Bags
	Cones
QB	Handoff
	Line spacing strip

1

FORM RUNNING AND AGILITY DRILLS

"There is a big difference between wanting to and willing to."

— author unknown

What Today Will Bring

"This is the beginning of a new day. God has given me this day to use as I will. I can waste it or use it for good. What I do today is important, because I'm exchanging a day of my life for it. When tomorrow comes this day will be gone forever, leaving in its place something I have traded for it. I want it to be gain, not loss; good, not evil; success, not failure. In order that I shall not regret the price I paid for it because the future is just a whole string of nows."

— author unknown

SPEED DEVELOPMENT AND AGILITY

The importance of speed and agility in the game of football cannot be over emphasized. The days of the slow non-athletic football player are gone. Today, coaches are sacrificing size in their players for speed and agility. That's why drills and techniques that actually help players improve in these areas are so important.

The primary phases involved in developing speed improvement are as follows:

1. Proper running technique
2. Flexibility
3. Sprint training
4. Overall strength training

PROPER RUNNING TECHNIQUE

When teaching form running, it is important to start with one technique and work on it first at half speed, work up to three-quarters speed, and finally, practice it at full speed. "Buzz" words, catchy words and phrases that go along with each technique, help players to better concentrate on the required skills.

To execute the following progressions of drills, put your players in four straight lines (approximately six to seven players across). They will remain in this order for the remainder of the form running/agility drills.

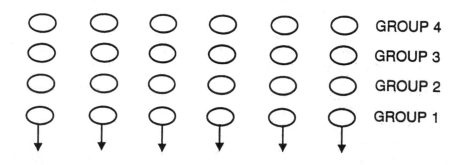

COACH

1 HAMMER DRILL

Purpose: To develop the proper upper body fundamentals involved in speed development.

Execution: The athlete stands with a slight forward lean, feet shoulder width apart. Eyes should be focused straight ahead and the arms should be in the locked position. On the coach's command, the athlete begins hammering his arms back at half speed for 15 seconds. The athlete takes a 15-second rest, and then begins a second set of arm repetitions at three-quarters speed for 15 seconds. The third and final set should be conducted at full speed to give the athlete the correct feel for rapid arm action with proper technique.

"Buzz Words:"

- "Focus" — Eyes should be focused straight ahead.
- "Pinch" — Fingers should form a loose fist with thumb on top of first finger.
- "Lock" — 90-degree bend in elbow.
- "Squeeze" — Palms should be turned inside, elbows should be close to the side.
- "Hammer" — Fist moves down through the pocket and past the butt, triceps should be parallel to the ground. The up hand should never pass the chin.
- "Rotate" — Arm action comes from rotation at the shoulder.

2 HIGH KNEES DRILL

Purpose: To develop proper running form with emphasis on quick high knee action. To develop hip flexor strength.

Execution: When the drill begins, each athlete will run 20 yards and back two times for a total of 80 yards. The coach will blow a whistle, signalling that each athlete is to run as quickly as he can while moving forward only gradually. Each repetition should be conducted at full speed and with an emphasis on quick high knee action while maintaining proper upper body technique. If the athletes tend to go forward too fast, slow them down. The athlete should be running on the balls of his feet with a slight body lean forward.

Variation: Low knees, quick hands, quick feet.

"Buzz Words:"

- "Drive" — Drive the knee up, feet should ricochet off the ground.

3 BUTT KICK DRILL

Purpose: To develop hamstring strength and quickness.

Execution: On the coach's signal, the players run 20 yards while maintaining proper upper body technique and concentrating on snapping their heels to the buttocks as quickly as possible. The athletes should maintain a slight forward lean while running. The drill should be repeated four times, with each repetition conducted at full speed.

Coaching Point: Emphasize quickness without moving forward too fast.

4 BOUNDING DRILL

Purpose: To develop explosive power in form running.

Execution: The athletes should run 20 yards and practice driving the knee to the chest while exploding off the back foot. As the players land on the other foot, they should explode up and drive the knee to the chest. Emphasis should be on explosion upward not outward. The athlete should still concentrate on proper upper body mechanics. Make sure athletes are not skipping, and that they emphasize explosion every time they hit the ground. Each athlete should run four times.

"Buzz Words:"

- "Explode" — Drive knee to chest and explode off the ground.
- "Hang" — The better the explosion, the better the hang time.

5 GERMAN KICK DRILL

Purpose: To develop proper leg mechanics in form running.

Execution: The athletes will cover 20 yards while concentrating on punching the knee out, not up, and snap the foot down. This is not a punting motion. The knee will lift naturally, punch out, and snap down. The drill should be repeated four times.

"Buzz Words:"

- "Punch" — outward knee movement
- "Snap" — snap foot down and back underneath hip

6 STANCE AND START DRILL

Purpose: To develop proper stance and starts when running sprints.

Execution: If the athlete is right handed, he should place his left foot as near to the starting line as possible, "crowding the line". He should also drop his right hand down in front of the line. The feet should be staggered with the majority of the weight on the front foot and hand. The back foot should not be extended too far back because the athlete wants to gain ground on his first step. His tail should be raised up with the off hand on the hip. On the starting count, the athlete should explode off the up foot, stay low and gradually work up into proper running form. After the player runs 20 yards, the finish line becomes the starting line. This drill should be repeated four times.

7 SEVEN-AND-A-HALF FOOT STRIDE DRILL

Purpose: To increase stride length in form running.

Execution: From their small groups, the athletes will cover 40 yards. The first row begins the drill by running with proper stance and start techniques. As they run, they should work to lengthen their stride while maintaining proper running form. If the drill is run on the football field, the athlete should work to take two steps every five yards.

Speed Improvement Variations:

Hill workouts (Sprints, cariocas, and backpedaling).

AGILITY DRILLS

The agility program included here consists of drills which relate to the game of football. The agility drills involve rapid change of direction, lateral movement, change of pace running, activities that force players to pick up their feet and drills to improve balance.

1 CARIOCA

Purpose: To improve hip flexibility

Execution: The athletes line up in three rows facing the coach. From their starting position, the athletes will "carioca" 20 yards in one direction, then back in the other directions. To carioca, the players face sideways with the shoulders square. They then run sideways, left foot over right and then left foot behind right while rotating the hips. The athletes will repeat the drill twice and keep an emphasis on staying low with shoulders square.

2 QUICK FEET CARIOCA

Purpose: To develop quick feet and improve hip flexibility.

Execution: The athletes line up in three rows facing the coach. From their starting position, the athletes carioca 20 yards in one direction, then back in the other direction. The athletes should repeat the drill twice, with emphasis on staying low, keeping the shoulders square, and taking short quick steps.

3 QUICK FEET

Purpose: To develop quick feet.

Execution: . The athletes line up in three rows facing the coach. From their starting position, the athletes take quick choppy steps laterally until coach signals them to sprint out past the coach . The emphasis should be placed on staying low and having quick feet.

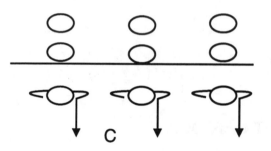

4 QUARTER EAGLES

Purpose: To develop quick feet and improve hip flexibility.

Execution: The athletes line up in three rows facing the coach. On the coach's signal, the players take quick choppy steps and "flip" their hips in the direction of the coach's signal and then return to base position. The athletes sprint out past the coach on the coach's command. The athletes should focus on quick feet and rotating their hips while keeping their shoulders square when executing this drill.

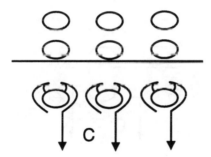

5 LATERAL SHUFFLE

Purpose: To develop athlete's ability to move laterally.

Execution: The athletes line up in three rows facing the coach. Upon the coach's signal, the athletes will lateral shuffle (shuffle sideways) in the direction indicated. Athletes fire out on coach's signal. The drill's emphasis should be on staying low and moving laterally without the athletes crossing their feet.

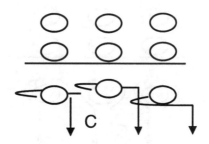

6 LATERAL WAVE

Purpose: To develop the ability to change direction.

Execution: The athletes line up in three rows facing the coach. Upon the coach's signal, the athletes turn and run in the direction of the coach's signal. The players should change direction on the coach's next signal and fire out on command. The coaches should stress the importance of staying low, planting, pivoting, and redirecting.

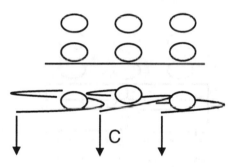

7 LINE DRILL

Purpose: To develop change of direction skills.

Execution: The athletes line up in three rows straddling the yard line facing the coach. On command, the athletes turn and run five yards, touch the yard line, and sprint 10 yards back in the direction from which they came, touch the yard line and sprint through the original starting line. The players should keep in mind the importance of staying low, planting the foot, and then accelerating to a sprint in the opposite direction.

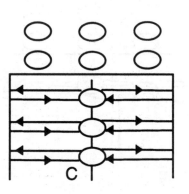

8 UP AND BACKS

Purpose: To develop backward run and change of direction skills.

Execution: The athletes line up in three rows facing the coach. On the coach's command, the athletes backpedal five yards, touch the line, plant, and drive. They should sprint to the original starting line, touch the line, and begin to backpedal. (For more information on backpedaling, please see the Defensive Back chapter.) The drill should be conducted for 30 seconds with an emphasis on staying low and perfecting change of direction skills.

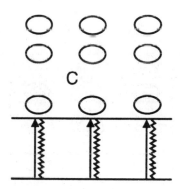

9 DOT DRILL

Purpose: To develop quickness of foot.

Execution: The athletes line up in three rows behind three sets of dots. Four of the dots form a square with each dot one yard apart and one dot in the center of the square. On the coach's command, the athletes put their feet on the first two dots, jump with both feet to the center dot, then jump out to put one foot on each of the dots on the opposite side of the square. The athlete will then hop back to the center dot, then to the original starting position (similar to hopscotch). The drill should be conducted for 30 seconds with an emphasis on keeping the feet close to the ground, the weight centered on the balls of the feet, and the body moving as quickly as possible.

Variation: Jump on one foot in a figure-8, work for 15 seconds on each foot.

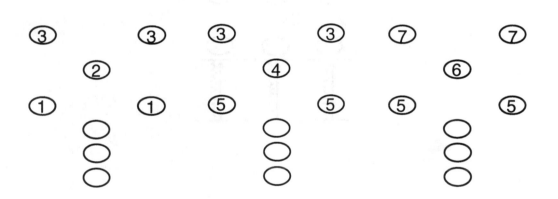

10 STEP DRILL

Purpose: To develop quickness of foot.

Execution: The athletes will line up on the stadium steps. On their coach's command, the athletes should step up with their right foot, then with their left, back down with their right foot then with their left. The drill should be conducted for 15 seconds, rest 15 seconds for four repetitions. The players should alternate lead steps and emphasize quickness.

11 LINE HOPS

Purpose: To develop quickness of foot.

Execution: The athletes line up in three groups on one side of a line. On the coach's command, each athlete crosses the line while hopping and keeping his feet together. The drill should be conducted for 15 seconds with four repetitions. The emphasis should be on keeping the weight on the balls of the feet and moving as quickly as possible.

12 WAVE DRILL

Purpose: To develop skills related to change of direction.

Execution: The athletes line up in three lines facing the coach. On the coach's command, the athletes sprint in the direction dictated by the coach (ie: right, left, backward, forward, or any diagonal direction). The athletes change direction by planting the outside foot and sprinting in the proper direction. The drill should be conducted for 15-20 seconds with four repetitions. The coach should stress the importance of staying low, executing proper change of direction techniques, and keeping the eyes on the coach.

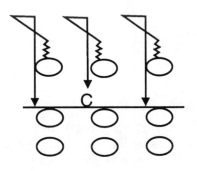

BAG DRILLS

Purpose: To develop foot agility and quickness.

Preparation: Position six dummies (bags) in a straight row one yard apart. Align two cones five yards from the end dummies. The athletes will line up single file behind a specified cone. During each progression, the athletes will sprint through the cones as they cross the final bag. Each drill should be executed in both directions for two repetitions.

Bag Drill Progressions

1 ONE FOOT IN THE HOLE

Execution: The athletes run through the bags with proper running form. During this drill, they should concentrate on picking up their feet.

2 TWO FEET IN A HOLE

Execution: The athletes run through the bags with proper running form with an emphasis on quick feet.

3 SHUFFLE DRILL

Execution: The athletes shuffle through the bags with emphasis on staying low and picking up their feet.

4 CARIOCA DRILL

Execution: The athletes carioca through the bags with emphasis on staying low, keeping their shoulders square, and picking up their feet.

5 SNAKE DRILL

Execution: The athletes should sprint to the top of the bag, backpedal to the other end, sprint, and repeat, weaving through the bags.

6 EXPLOSION DRILL

Execution: The athletes should keep their feet together and hop over the bags. The emphasis should be on exploding (jumping higher each time) as the players go over the bags.

ROPE DRILLS

Purpose: To develop quickness of foot and sense of balance.

Equipment : Ropes

Preparation: Position ropes on a selected line. Align two cones five yards from either end of the ropes. The athletes line up single file behind a specified cone. The emphasis of the drills should be on proper running form, staying low, and picking up the feet. As each athlete begins the drills, he should sprint through the cones. The drills should be executed for two repetitions and in both directions.

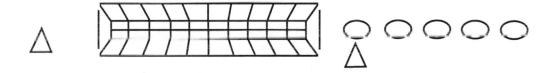

Rope Drill Progressions

1   ONE IN A HOLE

Execution: The athlete should step with the right foot in the right row of squares and the left foot in the left row.

2   EVERY OTHER HOLE

Execution: The athlete should step in every other square - right foot in the right row of squares and the left foot in the left row.

3   CRISS CROSS DRILL

Execution: The athlete should step in every other square, criss-crossing the feet - right foot in the left row and left foot in the right row.

4   SHUFFLE DRILL

Execution: The athlete turns and faces the coach. He works his way through the ropes by side stepping, placing each foot in each square using one row of the squares.

JUMP ROPE DRILLS

Purpose: To develop foot quickness, agility, and balance.

Preparation: The athletes form a circle around the coach. Each participant has a jump rope. Speed jumping should be emphasized in all drills.

Jump Rope Progressions

1 FIRST SET

Execution: The athlete jumps rope on left foot for 15 seconds working to get as many reps as possible. Rest 30 seconds.

2 SECOND SET

Execution: The athlete jumps rope on right foot for 15 seconds working to get as many reps as possible. Rest 30 seconds.

3 THIRD SET

Execution: The athlete jumps rope alternating feet (right foot, left foot) for 15 seconds working to get as many reps as possible. Rest 30 seconds.

4 FOURTH SET

Execution: The athlete jumps rope with both feet for 15 seconds working to get as many reps as possible. Rest 60 seconds and repeat all four sets two to four times.

CENTER - QUARTERBACK EXCHANGE DRILLS

"Success depends on adequate preparation and indomitable determination"

— author unknown

"THE MOST IMPORTANT FUNDAMENTAL IN FOOTBALL"

The center-quarterback exchange is the single most important fundamental in football. The snap begins the first phase of the offensive play. Without a proper exchange, the offensive unit seriously handicaps its ability for success. The center-quarterback exhange must be drilled over and over until all quarterbacks and centers develop a "feel" for one another. This phase of the offense must be perfect every time.

Basic Mechanics for the Center

1. The ball should be placed with its strings up or on the left side for a left handed quarterback.
2. The center's feet should be slightly wider than shoulder width.
3. The left hand is on the ground or resting on the thigh pad.
4. The right hand grips the ball, forming a "V" with the forefinger and thumb splitting the seam of the football.
5. Both heels should be slightly off of the ground.
6. The back is parallel to the ground with the head up.
7. Bring the ball up with the locked wrist in a pumping action.
8. Fill the top hand of the quarterback with the ball and force the fingers through.
9. Keep the rear steady when hitting out.

Basic Mechanics for the Quarterback

1. The quarterback stands in a parallel stance with the weight on the balls of his feet.

2. The knees should be slightly bent.

3. The right hand is wrist deep, the index finger should be placed in the middle of the center's rear.

4. The left hand should rest under and beside the right hand. (Thumbs should fit in natural grooves.)

5. The arms should be slightly bent.

6. As the ball is snapped, move with the center and close the left hand on the ball.

7. Bring the ball to the stomach and carry out the play.

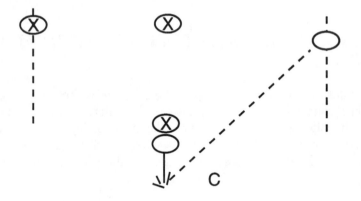

1 FILL THE HAND DRILL

Purpose: To see if the center is executing a proper snap.

Execution: The quarterback places his right hand underneath the center. The center executes the snap and works to fill the quarterback's hand. The quarterback lets the ball drop to ground. If the ball goes forward as it hits the ground, the center is too short on the snap. If the ball goes backward, the center is lifting the ball too deep. If the ball lands flat and bounces straight up, the center has executed a proper snap.

2 ON THE LINE DRILL

Purpose: To practice quarterback-center exchange against a defender.

Execution: Align all quarterbacks and centers on the selected line of scrimmage. A defender is positioned over each center, technique is dictated by coach. The quarterback selects play and cadence. On the cadence, the center snaps the football and executes the appropriate blocking scheme. The quarterback executes proper technique as designated by play.

Coaching Points:

1. Check for proper stances.
2. Check for proper ball exchange.
3. Make sure center is executing proper blocking scheme.

Variations:

- Three on the line.
- Offside snap drill.
- Wet ball snap drill.

3 CADENCE SNAP DRILL

Purpose: Execute proper techniques and fundamentals with the quarterback-center exchange.

Personnel: All centers and quarterbacks.

Execution: Align the centers and the quarterbacks four yards apart on a selected line of scrimmage. The coach designates a signal caller. The quarterback selects a play and a cadence. On the cadence, the centers snap the footballs and quarterbacks and centers execute proper techniques.

Coaching Points:

1. Check for proper stances.
2. Make sure quarterbacks are applying enough pressure.
3. The ball should make "pop" noise.
4. Make sure quarterback-center exchange is properly executed.

3
QUARTERBACK DRILLS

"Leaders have two important characteristics: first, they are going somewhere, and secondly, they are able to persuade other people to go with them."

— author unknown

DEVELOPING "GOOD HANDS"

As the quarterback handles the football on every play, it is imperative to run quarterback ball handling drills at every practice. Ball handling drills help develop confidence in the quarterback's ability to handle the football and the quarterback's hand-eye coordination. Because the strong hand receives the majority of the work in most drills, the following drills will focus on developing the weak hand. Repetitions and confidence in the quarterback's ball handling skills will reduce the number of bobbled snaps, hand offs, and the like, thus resulting in fewer turnovers.

1 RE-GRIP DRILL

Purpose: To improve ball control.

Execution: The quarterbacks grip the ball with the palm of their hand facing the ground. They move the ball up and down, making sure to re-grip the ball everytime. After a preset number of repetitions, the quarterbacks will switch hands and execute the drill with other hand.

2 BALL DROP DRILL

Purpose: To improve ball control.

Execution: The quarterback holds the ball in front of his body with an extended arm. He then drops the ball and re-grips it in the air. After re-gripping, the quarterback brings the ball back up to the original position and repeats the drill for a preset number of repetitions. Use both hands to execute this drill.

Variation: Use two footballs and execute the drill with both hands simultaneously.

3 DROP AND CIRCLE DRILL

Purpose: To improve ball control.

Execution: Follow the same procedure as the "Ball Drop Drill." As the quarterback drops the football, he attempts to circle the football and re-grip it in the air. He then brings the ball back to original position and repeats the drill. Practice this skill with both hands.

Variation: Use two footballs and execute the drill with both hands simultaneously.

4 FLIP DRILL

Purpose: To improve ball control.

Execution: The quarterback holds the ball at one end with the palm of the hand facing down. He flips the ball with his fingers to give it a full back flip so the ball lands on the back of the hand. The back of the hand hits the ball forward, causing a full front flip which returns it back to its original position. The quarterback then re-grips the ball and continues the drill. Execute the drill with both hands.

5 GLOBETROTTER DRILL

Purpose: To improve ball control.

Execution: On the coach's command, the quarterback begins passing the ball from one hand to the other: between the legs, behind the back, and other varieties, as quickly as possible. The drill should last about 30 seconds, the players should then rest and repeat as many sets as desired.

Variation: Execute the drill with the eyes closed.

6 STRENGTH DEVELOPMENT DRILLS

1. Wrist roller
2. Wrist curls
3. Reverse wrist curls
4. Tennis ball squeeze

Wrist Roller

Reverse Curls (one arm)

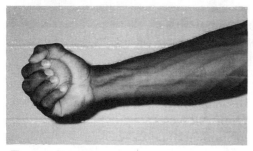

Tennis Ball Squeeze

Wrist Curls

PASSING TECHNIQUE — BASE MECHANICS

The Grip

The grip will vary depending on the size of the quarterback's hand, his release, and what seems most natural to him. The ball should be gripped firmly in a comfortable manner with the fingers spread and relaxed. Most passers will have at least two fingers across the laces. The index finger will usually extend up toward the nose of the football. There should be a slight gap between the ball and the palm for a consistent release. If the pass is thrown and the nose of the ball is down, the grip is too tight; if the nose goes up, the grip is too loose.

The Drop

As the quarterback retreats to his drop, he should grip the ball with both hands and elevate the ball to chest height. The quarterback should retreat as quickly as possible whether it be a three, five, or seven step drop. The ball is swung slightly from side to side for added balance.

The Stance

After the passer sets up to throw, he should have most of his weight on his back foot. His feet should be approximately shoulder width apart and the ball should be held around shoulder height.

The Off-hand and Arm

The primary functions of the off-hand are for it to serve as a guide to help control the football and produce a fluid throwing motion by rotating the shoulders and hips back and through. As the off-hand and arm come forward during the throwing motion, added force is gained during the rotation of the shoulders.

The Delivery

When throwing the football, the quarterback should take a short jab step in the direction of the throw. By taking a short stride, the quarterback is able to step quickly at two or three receivers as he scans the field.

The Release

The ball should be thrown either straight overhand or three quarters overhand. In releasing the pass, the ball should leave the index finger and possibly part of the middle finger. As the ball leaves, the hand should turn naturally with the thumb pointing downward.

The Follow-through

As the football is released, it is important that the quarterback follow through with the arm, shoulder, and hip to increase the velocity on the football. The correct follow-through is one that allows the body to transfer weight from one side to the other.

Coaching Points:

If the quarterback is having a hard time throwing spirals, you need to check for two possible mistakes:

1. Incorrectly gripping the football.
2. The ball should be leaving the index finger last — if it is leaving any other finger last, the player is putting too much pressure on the middle of the ball.

DEVELOPMENT DRILLS

1 KNEE DRILL

Purpose: To develop proper throwing action: wrist snap, arm strength, and quick release.

Execution: The quarterbacks face each other kneeling on the right knee (left knee if left handed passer) approximately five yards apart. When kneeling, the first player lifts the ball as if taking a snap and executes the proper throwing technique. The partner catches the ball and returns it, also using proper throwing technique. After a significant number of repetitions, move quarterbacks further apart – five yards back every ten repetitions.

Coaching Points:

1. Check to see if the quarterback has the proper grip.
2. Make sure the off-hand is in position to help secure the football.
3. Check the player's release - make sure football is leaving the index finger last.
4. Check his follow-through as well as accuracy.

2 HIP ROTATION DRILL

Purpose: To develop proper release and follow-through technique.

Execution: The quarterbacks stand 10 yards apart sideways with the point of their shoulders facing each other. The first quarterback throws the ball, making sure to rotate his hips and get his shoulder around. The second quarterback catches the ball and returns the first player's throw with the proper technique.

Coaching Points:

1. Check that athlete has the proper grip.
2. Make sure the off-hand and arm come forward during throwing motion.
3. Check for proper hip rotation.
4. Check for proper release technique.

3 ONE STEP AND THROW DRILL

Purpose: To develop proper delivery, release, and follow-through technique.

Execution: The quarterbacks stand 10 yards apart sideways with the point of their shoulders facing each other. Their feet should be approximately shoulder width apart with most of their weight on the back foot. The first quarterback takes a short jab step in the direction of the pass and executes proper release and follow-through technique. The second quarterback receives the ball and returns it to the first, using proper technique.

Coaching Points:

1. Check for proper grip.
2. Make sure each quarterback has taken a proper stance.
3. The quarterback should take a short jab step in direction of the pass.
4. Check for proper release and follow-through technique.

4 QUARTERBACK DROP DRILL

Purpose: To develop proper mechanics in the three, five, and seven step drops.

Execution: Align a quarterback with a football on a selected line of scrimmage in a pre-snap position. The coach designates a play with a three step drop. On the snap, the quarterback executes a three step drop and sets to pass. Repeat the three step drop for five repetitions. The coach then designates a play with a five step drop. The drill continues until the quarterback has had five repetitions with a three step drop, a five step drop, and a seven step drop.

Coaching Points:

1. Eliminate false steps - proper foot placement and weight transfer.
2. The quarterback should grip the ball with both hands.
3. The ball should be elevated to chest level.
4. Make sure the quarterback is getting into the drop as quickly as possible.
5. Check to see that the majority of the quarterback's weight is on the back foot when he sets up.

Variations:

- Include center-quarterback exchange.
- Time and record snap and drops.

5 CLOCK DRILL

Purpose: To develop proper drop and stance technique.

Execution: The coach tells the quarterbacks to execute a three, five, or seven step drop. On the cadence, the quarterback takes the proper drop. The coach calls out 12 o'clock, 9 o'clock, 3 o'clock, etc. , and the quarterback must step in that direction, pump fake, and step to the direction of the next call.

Coaching Points:

1. Emphasize the quick drop, securing ball with both hands.

2. Check to see if the quarterback is taking a short lead step or if he is over extending himself.

3. Make sure the quarterback is executing proper throwing mechanics.

Variation: Place receivers in these positions, and on the throw command, the quarterback releases the pass.

6   CIRCLE DRILL

Purpose: To develop the mechanics of passing a football on the run.

Execution: Align two quarterbacks 10 yards apart with one quarterback holding a football. On the coach's command, the two quarterbacks begin running clockwise in a circle, passing the football. After a certain number of repetitions, the coach will give a second command, and the quarterbacks will change direction and begin to run counter-clockwise, passing the ball back and forth. The drill continues until all paired quarterbacks have had a significant number of repetitions.

Coaching Points:

1. Emphasis should be placed on proper hip rotation and square shoulders.

2. Football should be secured by both hands, slight swagger for balance.

3. Emphasize quarterback leading the receiver while on the move.

7 SPRINTOUT DRILL

Purpose: To develop proper mechanics of passing a football on the run.

Execution: Use the yard lines at a 10-15 yard interval beginning on the sideline. The drill consists of two quarterbacks being assigned a yard line. The players run down their respective yard line, throwing the football to each other. When the quarterbacks reach the far sideline, they will turn around and continue the drill in the opposite direction. The tempo of the drill should be dictated by coach. The drill continues until all paired quarterbacks have executed a sufficient number of repetitions.

Coaching Points:

1. The football should be secured by both hands.,
2. The player's shoulders should have a light swagger for balance.
3. Be sure to place emphasis on proper hip rotation, square shoulders, and follow-through.
4. Emphasize the quarterback leading the receiver while on the move.

Variation: Use as an option pitch drill (use five yard interval).

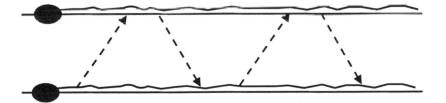

4

RUNNING BACK DRILLS

"A champion must have the desire for perfection and the will to punish himself in the process"

— author unknown

RUNNING BACK STANCE

Three-point Stance

Coaching Points:

1. Feet are shoulder width apart, staggered toe to instep.
2. Toes are positioned north and south with heels slightly off the ground.
3. Weight is evenly distributed on the balls of the feet and the down hand. The down arm is straight and supported on the finger tips. The off-hand rests on the thigh.
4. Shoulders should be square to the line of scrimmage and parallel with the ground.
5. The tail should be raised slightly above parallel to the ground.
6. The head is up and the eyes should be looking forward after checking defense and landmarks.

Two-point Stance

Coaching Points:

1. The feet should be parallel, shoulder width apart positioned north and south. Both feet should be flat, with weight slightly over the balls of the feet.

2. The knees should be bent while keeping body positioned over feet.

3. Both hands should be placed on the thigh pads, while keeping the shoulders square to the line of scrimmage

4. The eyes should be looking forward after checking defense and landmark.

1 STANCE AND STARTS

Purpose: To teach and develop proper stance and starts on a given cadence.

Execution: Align the running backs on a selected line. Teach the players the proper stances and critique them one at a time. Give running backs the play direction and snap count. On cadence, the players explode out of their stances and sprint 10 yards. Turn around, and execute the drill in the other direction. Plays should be run to both the right and left. The drill should continue until all players have had a sufficient number of repetitions.

Coaching Points:

1. Critique stance.

2. Players should take a short lead step in the direction that they are going.

3. Emphasize quickness, power, and staying low.

4. Change up cadence.

Variation: Practice three-point starts in the chutes.

BALL CARRYING

One of the most important factors for a successful offense is ball security. Players who have a problem handling the football usually find themselves sitting on the bench, collecting splinters. Ball security should be practiced every day whether your team is working in an individual period or in a team period.

The most important fundamental in ball security is holding on to the football. The nose of the ball should rest firmly in the fingers, locked between the index and middle fingers. Pressure is put on the back of the ball with the inside of the elbow and arm. As the ball carrier runs, the ball swings back and forth while maintaining constant pressure against the body.

Before contact, the off-hand should be placed over the top of the ball as the shoulders lower to deliver a blow.

1 BALL EXCHANGE DRILL

Purpose: To teach the proper technique in receiving a handoff and tucking the ball away.

Execution: Running backs form two lines 10 yards apart, facing each other. On cadence, the first running back takes off at 1/2 speed. The running back with the ball lays the ball out for a handoff. The running back receives the handoff and lays the ball out for next man in line. The next back in line does not take off until ball carrier receives the handoff. The drill continues until the running backs get a sufficient number of repetitions.

Coaching Points:

1. Receive hand off with inside arm up, folding down, and securing the ball with bottom arm – one fluid movement.

2. The running backs must develop a feel for the football, and keep the eyes straight ahead.

3. Make sure the running backs receive handoffs from the right and left position.

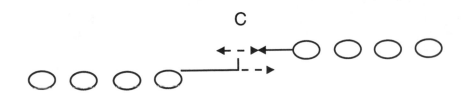

2 HANDOFF BAG DRILL

Purpose: To teach and practice the proper fundamentals in the execution of the handoff.

Personnel: Two quarterbacks and all of the running backs.

Execution: Align two rows of three blocking dummies (bags) five yards apart. There should be a one yard separation between each dummy (see diagram). Divide the quarterbacks and running backs into two groups aligned behind bags. The coach designates the cadence. On the snap both quarterbacks execute handoffs to the first running back in line. The running back secures the football and runs through the dummies. After the running back crosses the last bag, the coach will give a direction for the back to break. The running backs change lines after each repetition. The drill continues until all backs receive a sufficient number of repetitions.

Coaching Points:

1. Check running backs' alignment and stance.

2. Check to see that handoff technique is executed correctly.

3. Emphasize lifting the knees and ball security as the running back runs through the bags.

4. Make sure the running back makes a good sharp break after crossing the last bag in the proper direction.

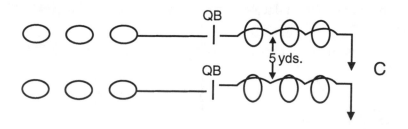

3 SPLIT THE BAG DRILL

Purpose: To teach running backs to receive handoff right before contact.

Execution: Set two bag holders side by side with the ball carrier three yards away. On the cadence, the running back runs a course to split the bags while the coach hands the ball off. The ball carrier receives the handoff and explodes upfield through the dummies. The drill should be conducted so that the running back receives the handoff from both right and left positions. The drill continues until all running backs get a sufficient number of repetitions.

Coaching Points:

1. Make sure the running back takes the handoff properly and secures the football.
2. Make sure the running back keeps his shoulders down and his butt low for leverage.
3. The player should explode through the bags, with good knee lifts and the feet in constant motion.
4. Bag holders have three options:

   • Both hit the ball carrier.
   • One hits the ball carrier.
   • Neither hits the ball carrier.

Variation: Place one defender five yards behind bag holders and have the ball carrier make a move off the defender.

4   GAUNTLET DRILL

Purpose: To teach ball security and running with leverage.

Execution: Place four to six men holding dummies approximately one yard apart, staggered. On the cadence, the running back runs through the gauntlet while coach hands the ball off. The running back receives the hand off and explodes upfield through "the gauntlet." The bag holders hit the ball carrier, trying to knock the ball loose and/or knock the ball carrier off-stride. The drill should be conducted with the running backs receiving handoffs from both right and left position. The drill continues until all of the running backs receive a sufficient number of repetitions.

Coaching Points:

1. Make sure the running back takes the handoff properly and secures the football.

2. Make sure the running back keeps his shoulders down and his butt low for leverage.

3. The players should explode through the bags, maintaining a good (high) knee lift and keeping the feet moving.

4. The player's goal should be to protect the football and stay on course.

Variation: Place one defender five yards behind the gauntlet and have the ball carrier practice moves to avoid being tackled.

5 TRIP DRILL

Execution: Defenders swing bags at ball carrier's feet trying to trip him.

6 RUNNING BACK PITCH DRILL

Execution: See "Pitch Drill" in chapter 9 (incorporate running backs).

Coaching Points:

1. Running backs should be instructed to look the ball in and secure the football before eyes go upfield.
2. Players should practice catching the pitch with two hands.

7 BAD PITCH DRILL

Purpose: To teach the running back proper fundamentals when receiving a bad pitch.

Execution: Same execution as the "Pitch Drill." The quarterback or running back is instructed to pitch the ball either behind the ball carrier or in front of him. This drill makes the ball carrier concentrate more on receiving the ball (ball security) before advancing the football.

OPEN FIELD RUNNING DRILLS

1 BALL SWITCH DRILL

Purpose: To teach ball security in open field running.

Equipment: Six cones and footballs.

Execution: Align six cones staggered, five yards apart (*see diagram*). The running backs line up single file behind the first cone holding footballs. On the coach's command, the first running back weaves through the cones, making 45 degree cuts. As the running back approaches the cones, he must switch the ball to the outside arm to protect himself from a would-be tackler. The drill should be taught at half speed and gradually increased as the running backs get a feel for the techniques. The drill should be conducted in both directions.

Coaching Points:

1. The outside arm should reach over the top of the football.
2. Both hands are used to guide the football to outside armpit.
3. The ball should be kept close to the body during the switch.
4. The inside arm should be used to protect the ball carrier against an oncoming tackler (cone).
5. Stress ball security.

2 STUMBLE DRILL

Purpose: To teach ball security and balance.

Execution: Line up the running backs with footballs on the goal line. On the coach's command, running backs begin running. At every five yard interval, the ball carrier must reach down and place the palm of his off hand on the yard line, causing him to stumble. The ball carrier regains his balance, switches the ball to opposite arm and executes stumble technique until he reaches the 25 yard line. After all running backs reach the 25 yard line, they should turn around and execute drill back to the goal line.

Coaching Points:

1. Players must place the palm of their hand on designated line.
2. Ball carriers should be instructed to raise their head up, stick their chest out and drive their knees forward to help them regain their balance.
3. Make sure the ball switch technique is executed properly.

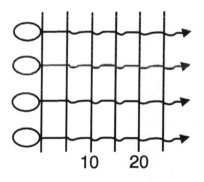

10   20

3 SIDELINE DRILL

Purpose: To teach ball security and balance while running down the sideline.

Execution: Align three bag holders five yards apart, three yards from the sideline. The coach and the running backs align on a selected line of scrimmage on the top of the numbers. On the snap, the coach turns and tosses the football to the running back. The ball carrier accelerates to the side line and works upfield. The running back must switch the ball to his outside arm and deliver a blow to the defender with his inside arm. This drill should be conducted in both directions. The drill continues until all running backs receive a sufficient number of repetitions.

Coaching Points:

1. Make sure running back has the ball secured in outside arm at all times.
2. Coach the running back to be the aggressor. He should not let the defender knock him out of bounds.

Other suggested drills:
    (For descriptions, see the Defensive Tackling Section.):

- Oklahoma Drill
- Four on Four
- Kentucky Gauntlet

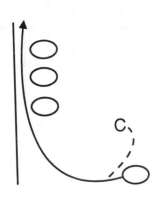

RUNNING BACK BLOCKING

Teaching Progression

1 FIT DRILL

Purpose: To teach running backs the proper blocking technique.

Execution: Divide running backs into two groups and pair them up on a selected line of scrimmage. Designate which side is offense and which side is defense. On command, running backs assume perfect fit position.

Coaching Points:

1. Players should keep the head up, flat back, butt down, good wide base and inside hand position.

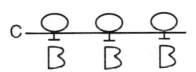

2 LOCK ON DRILL

Purpose: To develop skills related to staying locked on a defender.

Execution: One offensive player assumes the perfect fit position. On the coach's command, one defensive player will move in the direction indicated by the coach. The offensive player will lock on and maintain contact until whistle blows. This drill should be executed with one pair at a time.

Coaching Points:

1. Keep butt down and head up.
2. Fight pressure with pressure.
3. Step in direction of movement.

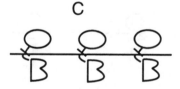

3 POPSICLE BLOCKING DRILL

Purpose: To teach proper blocking technique.

Equipment: One man sled (popsicle).

Execution: Align running backs in a single file line five yards behind popsicle sled. On cadence, the running back will explode out of his stance and make contact with the blocking sled. The running back will drive the sled for approximately five yards until the coach blows the whistle. The running back then goes to the end of the line and the next man in line steps up to execute the drill. The drill should be conducted until all running backs receive a sufficient number of repetitions.

Coaching Points:

1. Check for proper stance and starts.
2. The running back should keep his head up and shoulders square.
3. The running back should gather himself before contact.
4. When the running back makes contact with the sled, he should have a wide base and take short choppy steps.
5. Emphasize acceleration through the sled.

4 ISOLATION DRILL

Purpose: To teach the proper techniques and fundamentals in the execution of the isolation play.

Execution: Position offensive personnel (center, quarterback, fullback and tailback) on a selected line of scrimmage. Align four blocking dummies on the line of scrimmage two yards apart representing the two and three holes, (guard, center gap). Position two linebackers (right and left) four yards off the line of scrimmage holding blocking shields. The coach designates snap count and play direction. On the snap, the offensive personnel execute the isolation play. The fullback attacks the appropriate linebacker and drives him out of the play. The quarterback hands the ball off to the tailback, the running back follows the fullback up through the hole and breaks off the fullback's block. The drill should be conducted so the play is run to both sides.

Coaching Points:

1. Check for proper stance and alignments.

2. Instruct the front side linebacker to step up and attack the fullback.

3. The back side linebacker should scrape, while the center works to cut off the block.

4. Make sure all techniques and fundamentals in the execution of the isolation play are performed correctly.

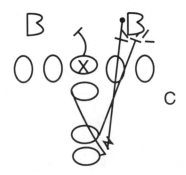

5 OFF TACKLE DRILL

Purpose: To teach the proper techniques and fundamentals in execution of the off tackle play.

Execution: Position offensive personnel (center, quarterback, fullback, and tailback) on a selected line of scrimmage. Align two blocking dummies on the line of scrimmage, representing the offensive tackles. Position two defenders representing defensive ends one yard outside the blocking dummy. The coach designates the snap count and play direction. On the snap, offensive personnel execute the off tackle play. The fullback attacks the defensive end attempting to kick him out. The tailback executes the proper footwork, receives the handoff and follows the fullback reading off his block. The drill should be conducted to both sides.

Coaching Points:

1. Check for proper stances and alignments.
2. Instruct the defensive end to attack the fullback with contained responsibilities or to come underneath the block.
3. Make sure all techniques and fundamentals in the execution of the off tackle play are performed correctly.

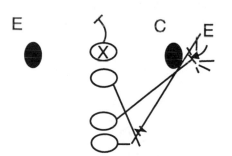

6 FULLBACK SWEEP BLOCK

Purpose: To teach the proper techniques and fundamentals in the execution of the toss sweep play.

Execution: Position offensive personnel (center, quarterback, fullback, and tailback) on a selected line of scrimmage. Align two cones on the line of scrimmage representing the tight end and offensive tackle position. Position two defenders on either side of the formation aligned anywhere between the corner position and the inside linebacker position. The coach designates snap count and play direction. On the snap, offensive personnel execute the toss sweep play. The fullback must adjust his course according to the alignment of the defender and the angle of support. The drill should be conducted so the fullback receives a sufficient number of repetitions blocking the support players in different alignments. The drill should be executed from both sides.

Coaching Points:

1. Check for proper stances and alignments.
2. The coach designates alignment and technique of defender.
3. Instruct the fullback to take a direct course towards the inside shoulder of the defender (get there as quickly as possible).
4. Make sure the fullback gathers himself before contact.
5. If the defender slow plays the block, instruct the fullback to kick him out.
6. If the defender attacks the fullback's block, execute a chop block through the outside thigh pad.
7. Instruct the tailback to stay deep and behind the fullback's block. He must read off the block and make the appropriate cut.

PASS PROTECTION

Running backs play a vital role in pass protection. They are often called upon to block on-rushing ends and blitzing line backers. They must have the ability to pass protect in order for the protection to be successful.

1 MIRROR DRILL

Purpose: To teach proper fundamentals and technique involved in pass blocking.

Execution: Align two cones five yards apart on a selected line of scrimmage. Position a running back and a defender two yards apart facing each other between the cones. On the coach's cadence, the running back will breakdown with his feet moving. The defender will move laterally between the cones as quickly as he can for approximately five seconds. The running back will mirror his movements without crossing his feet and keeping his shoulders square. After five seconds, the coach blows his whistle and the defender attempts to run by the running back. The running back steps up and executes a pass block. The drill should continue until all running backs receive a sufficient number of repetitions.

Coaching Points:

1. Instruct the running back to stay low with knees bent.

2. The running back should mirror defenders actions by sliding his feet against crossover steps.

3. As the defender attempts to rush, the running back should deliver a blow and stay locked on.

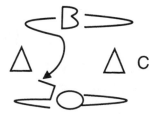

2 ONE-ON-ONE PASS PRO

Purpose: To teach proper technique and fundamentals involved in pass protection.

Execution: Position a line spacing strip on a selected line of scrimmage. Position a running back and a defender on a designated alignment. Place stand up dummy, representing quarterback drop. The coach designates the type of step (ie: three step, five step, or seven step) and snap count. On the snap, the defender executes pass rush technique. The running back executes pass block technique. The drill should be conducted so that running backs have the opportunity to block in both directions and have a sufficient number of repetitions.

Coaching Points:

1. Make sure running backs stay low and do not get over extended.
2. Running backs should mirror the defender's moves without crossing their feet.
3. Running backs should deliver blow and stay locked on.

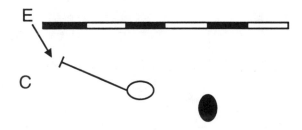

3 SPRINT-OUT DRILL

Purpose: To teach running backs proper sprint out blocking technique.

Execution: Position a line spacing strip on a selected line of scrimmage. Place running back and a defender on a designated alignment. Instruct the quarterback to sprint out in the appropriate direction. On the snap, defender executes contain rush technique. Running back executes sprint out pass block technique. The drill should be conducted to both sides and until all running backs have had a sufficient number of repetitions.

Coaching Points:

1. Instruct the running back to take an outside-in course on the defender.

2. The running back should drive his shoulder through the outside thigh pad of the defender and work to get his shoulders north and south.

3. Instruct defenders to protect themselves.

Other Suggested Running Back Receiving Drills:
For descriptions of these drills, please see the Group Pass chapter.

- Three on Three
- Individual Cuts
- Half-line Passing Drill
- Skeleton

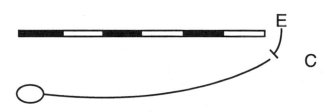

5

WIDE RECEIVER DRILLS

"The quitter gives an alibi; the mongrel, he gets blue. The fighter goes down fighting, but the thoroughbred comes through."

— author unknown

WIDE RECEIVER STANCE

Three-Point Stance - Sprinter's Stance

The receiver should position himself as if he were a runner in a starting block so that he can explode off the line of scrimmage. His feet should be shoulder width apart, with the outside foot dropped back with a heel to toe relationship. The outside hand is placed directly below the corresponding shoulder. His back should be straight and his shoulders should be parallel to the line of scrimmage. The inside arm should be placed with the hand on the outside of his thigh. His stance is rolled forward so that the majority of his weight is on his down hand and forward foot. This will help eliminate any false steps when he starts. His head should be up and his eyes looking downfield to survey the defense.

Two-Point Stance

The fundamental techniques of the two-point stance are the base technique used with the three-point stance. The feet should be shoulder width apart, the outside foot dropped back with a heel to toe relationship. The majority of the weight should be on the up foot. The back leg should be staggered naturally to give maximum power for exploding forward. The receiver should have a good body lean forward with the shoulders over the knees. The arms should hang in a relaxed manner. His head should be up with his eyes looking downfield to survey the defense.

Wide Receiver Releases

The ability to go deep is a receiver's most threatening weapon. His release should complement this threat by being explosive, forcing the defensive back to get deep in a hurry to lose his cushion. When the receiver makes himself a deep threat, he'll have the freedom to run any route because the defender won't be able to sit down and wait for the break.

The receivers should be taught to attack the defenders technique at full speed. When the receiver becomes head-up (directly across from the defender) on the defender, it allows the receiver to have a "three-way go" on him: he can beat him on the inside, outside, or by going deep.

No matter what release the receiver executes, it's imperative that he doesn't allow the defender to redirect him. An effective release is one that the receiver can avoid by the narrowest margin and get into his route as quickly as possible.

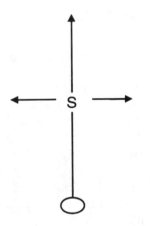

TECHNIQUE AGAINST A FREE RELEASE

Against a Three Deep Defender (Outside Technique)
Coaching Points:

1. The receiver should execute an outside release to gain a head-up relationship on defender.

2. The receiver should push the defender deep and get him back on his heels — close the cushion.

3. Make sure the defender does not dictate the depth of the receiver's route — inconsistent routes will throw off the opponent's timing.

Against a Two Deep Defender, Possible Man to Man (Inside Technique)

Coaching Points:

1. The player should execute an inside release to gain a head up relationship on defender.

2. You may apply the same coaching points as those used when attacking an outside technique.

Against a Head-up Defender

Coaching Points:

1. The player should release straight ahead.

2. You may apply the same coaching points as those used when attacking an outside technique.

When the defender rolls up on the receiver, it's imperative that the receiver's release is effective. The receiver cannot let the defender knock him off course and throw off the timing of the route. Two different types of releases against a rolled up corner may be taught.

Swim Technique

When used: Against coverage two or bump and run

Execution: The player will attack the defender's alignment. He should give a head or shoulder fake in opposite direction of release to get him overextended. (Note: defenders are taught to key the midsection of the receivers.) The goal of the receiver should be to get the defender to make eye contact with receiver so he'll bite on initial fake. The receiver should turn the shoulders slightly and step down the defender's hands with the inside hand. The receiver cannot allow the defender to get his hands on the front of his body. The receiver will then punch through with the outside arm over the inside shoulder of the defender, working all the time to get his hips beyond the defender. The receiver will then accelerate upfield and get into the proper route technique. The same technique can be used against an outside release.

Rip Technique

When used: Against coverage two or the bump and run

Execution: The receiver should attack the defender's alignment. He will give a head or shoulder fake in opposite direction of release to get the defender overextended. The receiver will then turn shoulders slightly and slap down the defender's hands with inside hand. The receiver will then rip through with outside arm, upper cut style, and turn the shoulders slightly in the opposite direction. The receiver should work to get his hips beyond the defender and accelerate upfield to get into route. The same technique can be used against an outside release.

1 RELEASE DRILL

Purpose: To teach proper release technique.

Execution: Pair up receivers on a selected line of scrimmage. Designate one line as receivers and the other line as defenders. Place a cone or a blocking dummy to designate the quarterback position. The coach instructs the defenders on their alignment and technique. The coach then specifies which route he wants to be executed. On the cadence, the receiver executes proper route release according to defenders alignment and technique. After each repetition, the two groups exchange responsibilities. Line one becomes the defenders and line two becomes the receivers. The drill should be conducted on both sides of the quarterback and against a variety of defensive looks.

Coaching Points:

1. Make sure receivers and defenders are aligned where they have enough room to execute drill.

2. Make sure receivers execute proper release technique.

BREAK POINT

The receiver always has the advantage over the defender because he knows where he's going on the field. This theory is correct as long as the receiver doesn't tip off his route. A defender looks for certain keys for recognition of the break point. When a defensive back recognizes the break point, he is able to settle and get a break on the ball. Such examples are a break in hurrying motion, short choppy steps, raised shoulders and the receiver's eyes going to the ground.

As mentioned earlier, the ideal situation is to teach the receiver to drive the defender off, which gives the illusion of a streak route. As the receiver gets within three or four yards of his break point, he should give a burst move to get the defender to open up. The receiver should now sink his hips, keep his shoulders over his knees, the head up, and the arms in normal running form. This will allow the receiver to have a low center of gravity and not tip off the break point.

The break itself is made off the opposite foot in the direction the receiver intends to go. The foot should be planted firmly in the ground with the knee bent, absorbing most of the force of the cut. After the cut, the receiver should be as near as possible to his correct line. The next step must be an acceleration step. This step will allow the receiver to create separation from the defender. The eyes and head should now be focused on the quarterback.

Catching the Football

The only way to become a better pass receiver is through repetition. A receiver must practice and be exposed to every type of catch so that he is prepared for any catch that happens in a game. Individual drills, group drills and team drills should be designed to enable the pass receiver to catch footballs in every type of situation.

The most important factor in proper receiving technique is concentration. From the time the eyes pick the ball up in flight until it is secured, the receiver's total concentration must be on the football. Emphasize two fundamentals — watch it in and tuck it away. The receiver's natural style will develop by emphasizing these two basic fundamentals.

The Passing Tree

It is a good idea to number all of the routes to simplify play calling and stay consistent in communication. The routes can be numbered one through nine as seen in the diagram below.

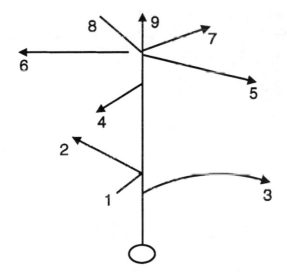

WARM UP DRILLS

(See also the ball handling drills in the Quarterback Drills chapter)

1 PEPPER DRILL

Purpose: To develop proper receiving skills and hand-eye coordination.

Execution: Align four wide receivers on a selected line of scrimmage facing one receiver five yards apart. Two footballs are used in this drill. One of the four wide receivers has one ball and the receiver in front has the other. The drill begins with the four wide receivers playing pitch and catch with the man out front. As soon as the man out front receives the pass, he throws it back looking for the next pass. After a sufficient number of receptions, rotate clockwise to give everyone an opportunity to be out front.

Coaching Points:

1. Emphasize proper receiving skills with the eyes and hands.

2. Make sure receivers don't throw the football until after the man out front has passed the ball to another receiver.

3. Repetitions are key in this drill.

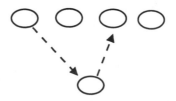

2 RECEIVER CIRCLE DRILL

Purpose: To develop proper receiving skills and hand-eye coordination.

Execution: Position five to six receivers in a circle with two footballs. The drill begins with receivers passing the ball around to each other. The balls move quickly within the circle so all receivers receive a sufficient number of receptions. (Note: the purpose of catching drills are to simulate as many types of catches as could possibly happen in a game situation so that a receiver feels comfortable with every catch.)

3 SQUARE IN DRILL

Purpose: To develop proper receiving skills.

Execution: The receivers align in a single file line on a selected line of scrimmage. On the cadence, the receiver will take two steps upfield, plant and come across the middle simulating a square in. The quarterback aligns approximately 10 yards from the receivers and throws the ball soon after the receivers break. After the reception, the receiver will tuck the ball away and turn upfield. After the first receiver executes the drill, he should form the next line to the right of the quarterback. The drill is conducted from both the right and left side. The drill should be run until all receivers have had a sufficient number of repetitions.

Coaching Points:

1. Receiver should look the ball all the way in; concentrating on the tip of the football.

2. The receiver should position his body so that he will catch the ball with his hands.

3. After the reception, the receiver should tuck the ball away and turn upfield.

Variation: Bag Drill — Position a defender holding a blocking shield approximately one yard deeper than the point of reception. Instruct the defender to hit the receiver with the shield as he catches the ball.

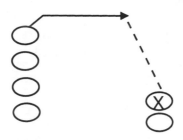

4 ONE HAND CATCH

Purpose: To teach the receiver to concentrate on the ball by making a one handed catch.

Execution: This drill is executed in the same fashion as as the "Square In Drill." The quarterback throws the ball so the receiver can catch it with his upfield hand. The receiver should tuck the ball away and turn upfield. The drill should be conducted so the receiver can practice one handed catches with both the right and left hand. The drill should be conducted until all receivers have had a sufficient number of repetitions.

Coaching Points

1. Emphasis should be on catching the ball with one hand out and away from the body.

2. Receivers must concentrate on the ball and look it all the way in.

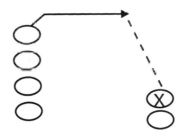

5 TURNAROUND DRILL

Purpose: To teach receivers to get head and eyes around to ball.

Execution: The receivers align in a single file line on a selected line of scrimmage with their backs to the quarterback. The quarterback will stand approximately 10-12 yards from the intended receiver. The quarterback throws the ball to the receiver and gives a "ball" call. The receiver then turns completely around, picks up the flight of the ball and makes the reception. The drill should be conducted so that the receivers practice right and left shoulder turns.

Coaching Points:

1. The drill teaches receivers to snap their heads around as they're coming out of their routes.

2. The drill helps develop hand-eye coordination and quick reflexes.

3. Make sure receivers turn completely around as they hear the "ball" call.

4. Make sure receiver executes proper ball receiving techniques.

6 CURL DRILL

Purpose: To teach proper techniques and fundamentals in the execution of the curl route.

Execution: Divide the receivers into two groups and align them in a single file line on a selected line of scrimmage (hash mark). Two quarterbacks will align approximately 10 yards behind the wide receivers in the middle of the field. On the cadence, the receivers will burst into the final two steps of their route, plant and come back to the ball. The two quarterbacks will throw to the designated receivers on each side. After the completion, the receiver should turn upfield and switch lines. The drill should be conducted until all receivers have had a sufficient number of repetitions.

Coaching Points:

1. The most emphasis should be on the break point. The receiver must burst out of his stance to give the impression of a deep threat.

2. As the receiver gets to the break point, he must sink his hips and plant off his outside foot. Check to see that receiver comes out of the break low, with square shoulders and always coming back for the ball. Eliminate wasted motion on break point. Check to see that receiver is executing proper ball receiving techniques.

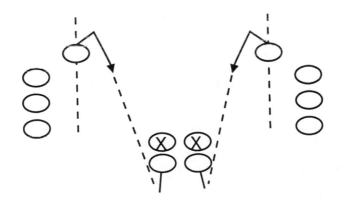

7 SIDELINE DRILL

Purpose: To teach receivers proper skills and fundamentals involved in catching a football near the sidelines.

Execution: Wide receivers will align in a single file line approximately five yards from the sideline. The passer stands 10-12 yards away from receiver. On command, the receiver will run to the sideline simulating the out route while the quarterback throws the ball. The receiver makes the catch with two hands while keeping both feet in-bounds. The drill should be conducted from both the right and left sides. The drill concludes after all receivers have had a sufficient number of repetitions.

Coaching Points:

1. Make sure the receiver executes proper receiving techniques.
2. The receiver must have control of the ball before he worries about his feet.
3. The receiver should over exaggerate the tapping of both feet each time he makes a reception.

Variations:

- One hand catch
- Quarterback throws high passes
- Quarterback throws low passes
- Receiver catches ball and turns up the sideline

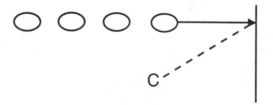

8 ENDLINE DRILL

Purpose: To teach receivers proper skills and fundamentals involved in catching a football in the back of the end zone.

Execution: Wide receivers will align in a single file line along the back of the end zone. Quarterbacks will stand approximately 15 yards away. On command, one wide receiver will run along the end line while the quarterback throws the ball high. The receiver must time his jump and make a two handed reception at the highest point. As the receiver comes down, he must work to get his feet down in-bounds. The drill should be conducted from both right and left sides. The drill concludes after all receivers have had a sufficient number of receptions.

Coaching Points:

1. Make sure receiver executes proper receiving techniques.

2. The receiver should catch the ball at its highest point.

3. The receiver should over exaggerate the tapping of both feet after each reception.

Variations:

- One hand catch.
- Quarterback throws low ball.

9 OVER THE SHOULDER DRILL

Purpose: To teach proper techniques and fundamentals involved in catching the football over the shoulder.

Execution: Divide receivers into two groups. Align the first group on the right hash mark. On the quarterback's cadence, the receiver executes a take off route. The quarterback takes a short drop and throws the ball over the outside shoulder of the receiver. The receiver makes the reception following the ball all the way into his hands. After the receiver executes the drill, he switches lines. The drill should continue until all receivers have had a sufficient number of repetitions.

Coaching Points:

1. The drill should be taught at ½ to ¾ speed.
2. Coach the receiver to position his body so that he will make the reception with his hands.
3. Emphasize to the receiver that he must follow the ball all the way into his hands as he makes an over the shoulder reception.

Variations:

- Same execution, but teach the receiver to turn his head around and relocate the ball over the outside shoulder.
- Same execution, but coach the quarterback to throw an under thrown ball and have the receiver come back to make the catch. (Coach the receiver to make the reception at the highest point possible.)
- See also "Pat and Go" in the Group Pass section.

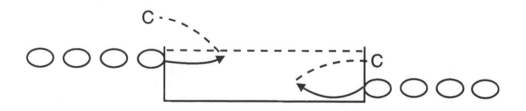

CONCENTRATION DRILLS

1 BLUR DRILL

Purpose: To teach receivers to concentrate on the football while having their vision obstructed.

Execution: Divide receivers into two groups on the sideline two yards apart. The coach stands approximately 8 to 10 yards away on the top of the numbers. The group in front is designated as the defender and the group in the back is designated as the receiver. On the coach's command, the defender and the receiver run parallel to each other. The defender harasses the receiver and obstructs his vision. The coach throws the football through the defender to the receiver. The drill should be conducted in both directions and until all receivers have had a sufficient number of repetitions.

Coaching Points:

1. Make sure receiver concentrates solely on the football and not the defender.

2. Make sure receiver executes proper receiving techniques.

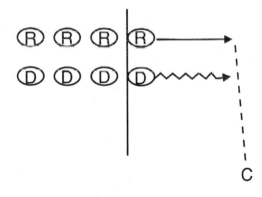

2 CROSSING DRILL

Purpose: To teach receivers to concentrate on the football while having their vision obstructed.

Execution: Divide the receivers into two groups facing each other on a selected line of scrimmage. One receiver will run across the field behind the defensive man crossing from opposite direction. The quarterback or coach will throw the ball to a point where the two players are about to cross. Instruct the defender to wave his arms and try to distract the receiver. The drill should be conducted in both directions and until all receivers have had a sufficient number of repetitions.

Coaching Points:

1. Receivers' concentration should be solely on the football and not on the defender.

2. Instruct the receiver to stay on the selected line of scrimmage and not to drift.

3. Make sure the receivers execute proper receiving techniques.

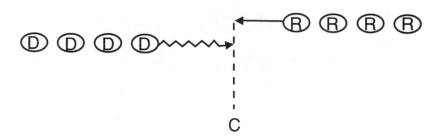

3 RECEIVER GAUNTLET DRILL

Purpose: To teach the skills related to receiving and ball carrying.

Execution: Align receivers on a selected line of scrimmage and a quarterback approximately 15 yards away. Position two dummy holders staggered five yards inside and five yards deep from the intended receiver. Align a third bag holder approximately five yards beyond the two dummy holders. On cadence, the receiver will execute a short route. The quarterback sets quick and throws to the intended receiver. As the receiver makes the reception, he then splits the two dummy holders and puts a move on the final bag holder. The drill should be conducted in both directions and until all receivers have had a sufficient number of repetitions.

Coaching Points:

1. Instruct the two dummy holders to hit the receiver as he makes the reception.

2. Make sure receiver is concentrating on the football and not the defenders.

3. Make sure receiver is executing proper receiving technique. The receiver should look the ball all the way in and secure it before contact.

4. The receiver should explode through the bags and put a move on the final dummy holder.

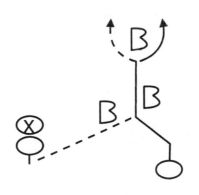

4 FULL GAUNTLET

Purpose: To teach the fundamentals of catching the ball and tucking it away before contact.

Execution: Position players in two parallel lines facing each other approximately two yards apart. The first receiver stands at one end approximately five yards away. On the cadence, the receiver runs toward the gauntlet, receives the pass, tucks the ball away and runs through the gauntlet. Instruct players on both sides to try to pull the ball away from the ball carrier. The drill should be conducted in both directions and until all receivers have had a sufficient number of repetitions.

Coaching Points:

1. Make sure receiver executes proper receiving techniques.

2. Emphasize holding on to the ball and use of good body control.

3. See also the "Quick Game," "Individual Cuts," and "Skeleton" drills in the Group Pass section.

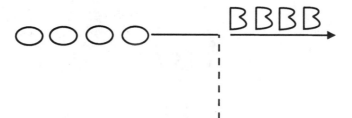

RECEIVER BLOCKING

The most important factor in receiver blocking is desire. Some receivers feel their only responsibility is to catch touchdown passes. The reality of sticking their noses into defenders turns them off. Good offensive running attacks include receivers that are willing to block and to do so aggressively. There are three different types of blocks that may be taught to receivers:

1. Stalk block
2. Chop block
3. Crack block

The stalk block is the block our receivers execute most often. As the ball is snapped, the receiver should drive off the line of scrimmage as if the play were a passing play. As he gets within three yards of the defender, he should break down under control, maintaining a low center of gravity and a wide base and taking short, choppy steps. His eyes should be focused on the target and in position to react and adjust. The receiver should initiate the contact, not absorb it. As contact is made, the receiver should work for inside hand position and apply pressure where he feels pressure. As the defender attempts to get to the ball, the receiver should increase the pressure and drive the defender. It's important that the receiver maintain a good base; he should not cross his feet at all, if possible.

As the ball carrier and the pursuit get closer to the stalk blocker, the receiver should execute a chop block. This technique serves two purposes: the defender has a hard time getting to the ball carrier when his feet are tangled up, and it helps reduce injuries to receivers who get trampled from behind.

The chop block is used as a change up against a hard-charging defender. The approach is the same as the stalk block, but at the last second, the receiver will lower his center of gravity and drive his shoulder through the knee of the defender. After the defender hits the ground, the receiver should get back on his feet and position himself between the defender and the ball carrier.

The third blocking technique used frequently is the crack block. The crack block is used to seal a linebacker or safety inside. On the snap of the ball, the receiver's eyes must go to the target. The receiver should come down the line of scrimmage under control with his shoulders parallel to the sideline. All adjustments to the defender's course should be made above the waist and with the receiver's head in front of the defender's body. The receiver will accelerate into the defender in the last five yards. His responsibility is to wall off the defender from the outside while executing the same fundamental described in the stalk block.

Receiver Blocking drills are broken down in the same manner as every other blocking drill:

1. Approach
2. Contact
3. Follow through

1 FORM FIT DRILL

Purpose: To teach proper stalk block technique.

Execution: Divide receivers into two groups on a selected line of scrimmage facing each other. The coach designates one group as the blockers and the other group as the defenders. On command, the blockers assume the perfect block position. The coach critiques each player, one at a time. Switch personnel and execute perfect block position with the second group.

Coaching Points:

1. Check for the following: head up, butt down, good wide base, good power producing angles in the legs, and inside hand position.

2 LOCK ON DRILL

Purpose: To teach receivers to lock on defender as he attempts to release.

Execution: Divide receivers into two groups on a selected line of scrimmage facing each other. On the coach's command, the defensive man will move in the direction indicated by the coach. The offensive player will lock on and maintain contact until the whistle blows.

Coaching Points:

1. Check for the following: head up, butt down, and a good base.

2. Receiver should fight pressure with pressure.

3. No crossover steps, keep a base beneath the body.

4. See also: "Mirror Dodge Drill" (Offensive Line Section).

C

3 STALK BLOCK DRILL

Purpose: To teach proper technique and fundamentals involved in the stalk block.

Execution: Divide receivers into two groups and designate one group as the blockers and the other as the defenders. Align the first blocker on a selected line of scrimmage and the first defender five to seven yards off the line of scrimmage. The defender holds a hand shield, back pedals a short distance and breaks forward in one of three directions. The receiver will break down under control making contact with the shield and execute a stalk block. The drill should continue until all receivers have had a sufficient number of repetitions.

Coaching Points:

1. Make sure receiver breaks down under control, uses proper footwork and delivers a blow at the point of contact.

2. The drill should be conducted at ½ to ¾ speed.

4 STALK BLOCK AGAINST THE DEFENSIVE BACKS

Purpose: A full speed drill to teach proper techniques and fundamentals involved in wide receiver blocking against secondary support.

Execution: Divide receivers and defensive backs into two groups on each side of the field. Position a quarterback in the middle of the field and use backup receivers and backup defensive backs as ball carriers. Position two cones 10 yards apart on both sides of the field on either side of the receiver. The coach instructs the defensive back which technique to play. On the cadence, the quarterback tosses the ball to the running back. The running back runs ¾ speed between the cones. Receiver executes stalk block against a defensive back. The defensive back attempts to defeat the block and form up on the ball carrier. The drill should continue so all receivers and defensive backs have had a sufficient number of repetitions.

Coaching Points:

1. Make sure receivers execute proper blocking technique.

2. Receiver should use chop block as a change up.

3. Good competitive drill for receivers and defensive backs.

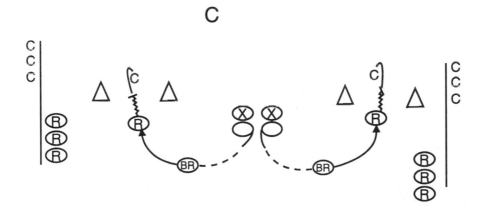

6

OFFENSIVE LINE DRILLS

"The credit belongs to the man who is actually in the arena; whose fate is marred by dust and sweat and blood; who errs and comes short again; who knows the great enthusiasms, the great devotions, and spends himself in a worthy cause; who at best knows in the end the triumph of high achievement; and who at the worst, if he fails, at least fails while daring greatly, so that his place shall never be with those cold and timid souls who know neither victory nor defeat."

— Theodore Roosevelt

OFFENSIVE LINE STANCE

A proper stance is extremely important to an offensive lineman and should be as nearly perfect as possible. The stance will enable the lineman to get to his point of contact with the necessary leverage and power required to defeat the defender.

Stance Coaching Points

The feet should be spread at least armpit width, never wider than shoulders, with a toe-to-instep relationship. The toes should be pointing straight downfield (don't tip off the blocking scheme). After establishing the proper foot relationship, instruct the lineman to drop into a squatting position and extend the down hand slightly inside the near foot, forming a tripod. The weight should be distributed between the ball of the feet and the down hand in a 60-40 ratio. The off hand should rest comfortably above the knee, shoulders should be square to the line of scrimmage and parallel to the ground. The back should be flat with the tail at shoulder level or slightly higher. The lineman's head should be cocked back slightly with little or no strain on the neck muscles. His vision should include any defensive line or linebacker in his area.

As the lineman perfects his stance, it enables him to develop power producing angles. These power producing angles are created by the bend in the ankle and knee joints (Z in the knee) and the weight on the balls of the feet.

Starts

The lineman's objective is to create force when he comes out of his stance, so it is imperative that his initial movement is forward, not upward. In order for the blocker to maintain a power base, he must step with the appropriate foot. There are two simple rules for the first step:

1. Defender over — drive off the up foot and step with the rear foot.
2. Defender on either side — step with the foot nearest him.

1 START DRILL

Purpose: To teach proper stance and start technique for offensive lineman.

Execution: Align offensive linemen on a selected line of scrimmage. The coach designates block and cadence (ie: base block on one). On the snap count, the offensive linemen fire out over the air.

Coaching Points:

1. The player should mentally shift weight to the up foot and step with rear foot.
2. The first step should replace the down hand to maintain base and not be an over or under stride.
3. The player should roll over up foot, knee should be pointing to the ground.
4. The player should keep a flat back and the head up.
5. The first step should be followed quickly by the second and third steps.
6. Emphasize staying low and hitting out.

THE THREE PHASES OF OFFENSIVE LINE BLOCKING

The offensive line blocking technique consists of three phases:

1. Approach
2. Contact
3. Follow through

When teaching blocking, it is helpful to teach the progression in the following order: contact, follow through, approach.

Fit Position (contact phase)

Purpose: To teach ideal blocking position utilizing power producing angles.

Execution: Put the blocker in a "perfect fit" position on the defender. The defender is in a two point stance, crouched low with arms in a catching position.

Coaching Points:

1. Feet parallel, good bend in knees and ankles (Z in the knees for power producing angles).
2. Butt down and back arched.
3. Head up with eyes in the numbers.
4. Hand placement - the palm of hands should be at the bottom of the defender's breastplate, elbows in near the chest.

Fit Follow Through (follow through phase)

Purpose: To teach proper use of leverage, hip roll and follow through when executing a block.

Execution: The offensive linemen will align in the fit position with the defender in a two point stance giving resistance. On the coach's command, the blocker will roll his hips and accelerate his feet. The blocker will continue to drive defender back until coach blows whistle. The blocker and defender stop, and the coach checks for proper follow through technique.

Coaching Points:

1. Check for proper technique in fit position.

2. Check for hip roll and acceleration of feet.

3. The blocker should keep a proper base underneath himself at all times to prevent over extension.

One Step Contact (approach phase)

Purpose: To develop proper approach and contact mechanics.

Execution: Put the blocker in the perfect fit position and tell him to take one step back. Place the defender in a two-point stance, crouched low with arms in a catching position. On command, the blocker explodes into the defender executing proper contact mechanics.

Coaching Points:

1. The face and hands should hit simultaneously.

2. The blocker should roll hips up and through defender.

3. The defender's head and shoulders should snap back and up.

1 ONE STEP CONTACT AND FOLLOW THROUGH

Purpose: To teach proper technique in the approach, contact and follow through phases of blocking.

Execution: Put the blocker in perfect fit position and have him take one step back. Place the defender in a two-point stance, crouched low with arms in a catching position. On command, the blocker explodes into the defender, rolls his hips and drives the defender straight back. The defender should give full resistance as he is being driven back.

Coaching Points:

1. The face and hands of the blocker should hit simultaneously.
2. Check for hip roll and feet acceleration.
3. Blocker should keep a wide base with toes pointing upfield taking short powerful steps.

2 HIT AND DRIVE DRILL

Purpose: To teach and practice all phases involved in the execution of the base block.

Equipment: Chutes and Boards

Execution: Align the offensive blocker under the chute in a three-point stance standing at the edge of the board. Place the defender one foot away in a two-point stance. (As the drill progresses, move the defender into a three-point stance.) On the cadence, the blocker will fire out of his stance and drive the defender down the board. The defender will collide with the blocker and give resistance as he is being driven back. As the drill progresses, vary the distance between the blocker and the defender.

Coaching Points:

1. Vary the cadence.
2. Check for proper stance and start technique.
3. Make sure blocker fires out and not up.
4. Check for three point contact (hands and face hitting simultaneously).
5. Check for hip roll.
6. Emphasize good base and acceleration of feet.

3 LOCK ON DRILL

Purpose: To teach the blocker to maintain contact in the follow through phase of blocking.

Execution: Use the same execution as the "Hit and Drive" drill. When the defender reaches the end of the board, the coach will give a direction to spin. The blocker must continue to fight pressure where he feels pressure, lock on, and finish the block.

Coaching Points:

1. Check for proper blocking technique.

2. As the defender tries to disengage, the blocker must step with the near foot in the direction of the spin and continue to drive the defender back.

3. The blocker should never cross his feet or put his heels together — keep a good base.

4 BASE BLOCK AGAINST A SHADE ALIGNMENT

Purpose: To teach base block technique against a defender aligned in a shade technique.

Execution: Same as "Hit and Drive" drill, except the blocker will start from a position with the inside foot on the outside of the board. On the snap, the blocker executes a base block driving defender through the chute. The players should practice blocking inside and outside chutes.

Coaching Points:

1. Vary the cadence.

2. Check for proper stance, start, and blocking techniques.

3. The blocker should mentally shift the weight on pressure foot.

4. The blockers first directional step must enable him to block the defender down the middle.

5. The second step must be upfield to maintain base.

SLED DRILLS

1 ONE-MAN DRIVE

Purpose: To develop leg drive.

Equipment: One-man sled.

Execution: Align linemen in a single file line in front of the one-man sled. The first lineman aligns himself an arm's distance away from the sled. On the coach's command, the lineman explodes into the pad and executes a base block. The sled must be driven in a straight line. On the coach's command, the lineman does a seat roll and sprints five yards, then returns to the end of the line. The next man in line steps up and executes the drill.

Coaching Points:

1. Check for proper stance.
2. Vary the snap count.
3. Check for correct first step and explosion into the pad.
4. Emphasize maintaining a wide base with short, choppy powerful steps while moving the sled.

2 TWO-MAN HIP ROLL

Purpose: To develop hip roll and full extension of the body.

Equipment: Two-man sled

Execution: Align linemen in two rows in front of the two-man sled. The first lineman in each row aligns himself an arm's distance away from the sled. On the coach's command, each blocker attempts to move the sled as far as possible with the forward thrust of his hips while not moving his feet. After the lineman has executed a hip roll, he will roll out and sprint five yards then return to the end of the opposite line. The next two men step up and execute the drill.

Coaching Points:

1. Vary the cadence.
2. Check for proper stances.
3. Linemen should explode out of their stances without bringing their feet together.

Variation:

- Two-man drive.
- Two-man hip roll executed two times in a row.

3 TWO-MAN DRIVE AND ROLL

Purpose: To develop leg drive after contact.

Equipment: Two-man sled

Execution: Align linemen as they were aligned in the two-man hip roll drill. On the coach's command, each lineman explodes into the pad, hitting it with his inside shoulder and driving the sled in a straight line. On the coach's next command, each lineman does a seat roll and blocks another lineman holding a dummy five yards from the sled. The lineman blocking the dummy now becomes the dummy holder and the dummy holder returns to the end of the row on the opposite side. The next lineman in each row steps up and executes the drill.

Coaching Points:

1. Check for correct stances.

2. Emphasize get-off and proper position of body when drive blocking.

3. Lineman should take short, powerful steps while maintaining a wide base.

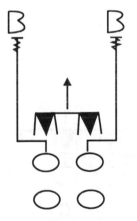

4 FIVE-MAN DRIVE

Purpose: To develop get-off and drive block.

Equipment: Five-man sled

Execution: The first unit forms a huddle six yards from the sled and receives a starting count from the coach. On the starting count, the players will execute a shoulder block and drive the sled; all linemen will block with the same shoulder. On the coach's command, players sprint out laterally. (When executing a left shoulder block, players sprint out to the right and the opposite for a right shoulder block.) As soon as the first unit leaves the sled, the second unit forms a huddle six yards behind the sled.

Coaching Points:

1. Stress quickness out of the huddle.
2. Check alignments and stance.
3. Vary the snap count.
4. Block both left and right shoulders.
5. Check to see that proper blocking technique is executed.

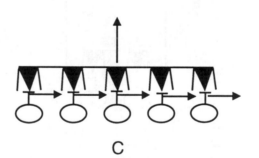

C

5 FIVE-MAN REACH

Purpose: To teach explosion and drive using the reach block technique.

Equipment: Five-man sled

Execution: Use the same set up as the five-man drive except when aligning on the sled, offset to the left or right edge of the pad depending on the direction of the reach block. On the starting count, the players execute the reach block and drive the sled. On the coach's next command, the linemen sprint out laterally (all in the same direction). As soon as the first unit leaves the sled, the second unit forms a huddle six yards behind the sled.

Coaching Points:

1. Stress quickness out of the huddle.
2. Check alignments and stances.
3. Vary the snap count.
4. Work both sides of reach block.
5. Make sure linemen are hitting correctly at point of contact and driving the sled in a straight line.

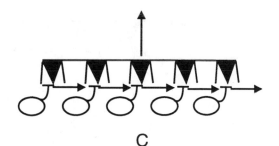

C

6 FIVE-MAN SEAT ROLL

Purpose: To teach explosion and agility.

Equipment: Five-man sled

Execution: Position linemen on the left side of the sled in a single file line. The first lineman steps up and gets into a three-point stance. On the coach's command, the first lineman will explode into the pad with his inside shoulder, recover using a seat roll, and then move to the next pad in the direction of the drill. The next lineman on the line will quickly get into a three-point stance in front of the first pad. The coach will give a command and both linemen will explode into the pads, recover with a seat roll, and move to the next pad in the direction of the drill as the next lineman on line gets into a three-point stance. The drill continues until the last lineman has reached the far end of the sled.

Coaching Points:

1. Stress correct hitting techniques.

2. Stress explosion and immediate recovery.

3. Drill should be conducted in both directions.

C

PASS PROTECTION

The primary objective of the offensive line in passing situations is to protect the quarterback. The success of the protection can be measured by the number of quarterback's passes that are thrown without pressure and without obstruction. Linemen must accept the responsibility of providing whatever time is necessary to get the ball off.

Adjustments must be made in body position and technique in the transition from run blocking to pass blocking. Pass protection requires the use of different abilities from those needed to run block. Run blocking uses forward leg drive and hip roll, while pass blocking requires the use of lateral and backward movements.

Pass blocking technique is broken down into five phases:

1. Pre-snap read

2. Set up

3. Punch

4. Body position

5. The finish

The pre-snap read is the first phase of pass protection. The lineman should know where the quarterback is setting up and his assignment according to the alignment of the defense. If blocking a down lineman, he should recognize his alignment and what he does from that alignment. If the defense is showing a blitz, he should be aware of his blitz pick-up responsibilities.

The next phase of pass protection is the set. The manner of setting varies depending on the alignment and capabilities of the opponent in accordance to the drop of the quarterback. (Linemen should know quarterback drops in steps and yards.) The goal of the set is for the lineman to position himself between the rusher and the passer as quickly as possible and as close to the line of scrimmage as possible. Getting there and then maintaining proper foot, body, and head position is the basis for getting the job done. The lineman should anticipate the snap count and get from a three-point to a two-point stance as quickly as possible. The lineman should bend his knees, arch his back, keep his head up and snap his arms up into the punch position.

The third phase of pass protection is the punch. One of the best methods of teaching this phase is to have the lineman punch with the butt of his hands inside the framework of the defenders body, and to aim for the base of the numbers on their jersey. The lineman should punch on the rise, working up through the man and work for a lockout position. They should remember to fight pressure with pressure and always keep between the rusher and the quarterback. The ability to move back as well as laterally is critical in pass blocking.

Linemen must also be able to position their body with their weight low and forward to maintain balance. The blocker should never let the defender get into his body and force him into an upright position. If the blocker's body position becomes upright, he'll lose the ability to control the defender. The lineman must work to keep separation from the defender while maintaining a proper base beneath his body. In order to keep a base, the lineman must have the ability to slide or shuffle his feet quickly without crossing over.

The final phase of pass protection is the finish. The majority of pass plays require protection for approximately four seconds to get the pass off. Occasionally, breakdowns within the offense may require longer protection. Linemen must accept the responsibility of providing whatever time necessary to get the ball off. The players must never quit. They should stay after the defender until the whistle blows.

Passing Pocket

The pocket is an area from a depth of three to four yards to the width of the offensive tackle's outside shoulders. The guards are responsible for maintaining the depth of the pocket and the tackles are responsible for the width of the pocket.

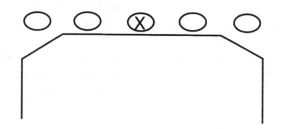

Pass Protection Progression

When teaching pass protection, it is a good idea to begin with two linemen working with each other. The drills offered teach the progression in order of the set, punch, body position and finish.

1 SET UP DRILL

Purpose: To teach proper technique for the set position
(Note: drill is executed with only one lineman.)

Execution: The lineman takes correct three-point stance. On the coach's command, the lineman takes a quick step back with the inside foot, shuffles the outside foot to parallel position. The weight will shift back, the butt drops and the hands are snapped up to a point just below the eyes. The lineman's head is up and the elbows should be inside the shoulders.

Coaching Points:

1. Make sure the players are in the correct three-point stance, don't let them tip the defense by having their weight back.

2. Stress quick movement with the eyes on the defender.

3. The blocker should have his weight evenly distributed with the feet no wider than shoulder width apart.

2 PUNCH DRILL

Purpose: To teach the correct method of delivering a blow when pass blocking.

Execution: Pair up offensive linemen on a selected line of scrimmage. The blocker aligns in a three-point stance with the defender in a challenge position. On the coach's command, the blocker sets up in the proper pass protecting position. From the set position, the blocker will punch the defender using proper technique. The drill should be conducted so that all linemen receive a sufficient number of repetitions.

Coaching Points:

1. Check stance. Stress a quick and proper set.

2. The punch should be made with the butt of the hands to the inside framework of the defender's body.

3. Make sure contact is made at the base of the defender's body.

4. Make sure the lineman is not lunging. Only the hands and arms should move out, not the body.

5. Linemen should work for a lockout position. The head should be up, butt down, and feet in a good balanced stance.

3 BODY POSITION DRILL

Purpose: To teach proper body position in pass blocking.

Execution: The defensive man aligns in a challenge position with his hands grabbing the shoulders of the blocker. The blocker assumes the proper lock out position. Align a cone in the backfield representing the quarterback's drop. On the coach's command, the blocker shuffles his feet, maintaining an inside position as the defender moves side to side and toward the passing point. The drill should be conducted so that all linemen receive a sufficient number of repetitions.

Coaching Points:

1. Check to see that the linemen begin the drill in a proper lock out position.

2. The blocker should slide his feet as quickly as possible to maintain body position. The more the feet are in contact with the ground, the quicker the blocker can adjust to the defender.

3. Make sure the blocker maintains proper body position – he should not get over extended.

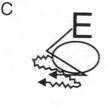

4 FINISH DRILL

Purpose: To teach an awareness of where to take the defender in accordance with the passing point.

Execution: Pair up offensive linemen on a selected line of scrimmage. Align a stand up dummy in the backfield representing the quarterback's drop. The defensive man aligns over offensive lineman. On the coach's command, the blocker sets up, punches and maintains proper body control against the defender's rush. The blocker must now know where the passing point is in order to finish the block.

Coaching Points:

1. Make sure the lineman executes proper pass protection techniques.

2. The blocker must keep the defender from the stand up dummy until the whistle blows.

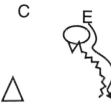

5 SEVEN-MAN SLED

Purpose: To teach proper body position, punch, and lockout skills during pass protecting.

Equipment: Seven-man sled

Execution: Position the lineman on one side of the seven-man sled. The first lineman gets into a proper stance facing the first pad. On the coach's command, the lineman sets up and punches the pad. The lineman must punch, lock out, clear, and shuffle to the next shield. The drill continues all the way down the sled. The drill should be conducted in both directions and until all linemen have had a sufficient number of repetitions.

Coaching Points:

1. Check for proper stance and set ups.

2. Make sure linemen are executing proper punch and lockout techniques while maintaining correct body position.

3. Check for over extension.

4. Linemen should shuffle with quick feet between each pad.

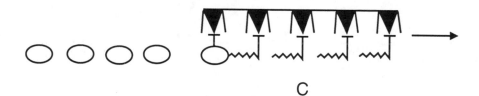

C

6 MIRROR DODGE DRILL

Purpose: To teach proper position, balance, and lateral movement while pass blocking.

Execution: Divide linemen into two groups and have them pair up. Two cones are placed five yards apart and one yard off a selected line of scrimmage. The lineman gets into his stance with his hand on the line. Position the defender in a two- or three-point stance directly across from the offensive lineman. On the cadence, the lineman sets up and punches. The defender attempts to run past the blocker between the cones. The lineman mirrors the defender's moves and punches to a lock out position. The defender continues to work moves until the whistle blows. The drill continues until all linemen have had a sufficient number of repetitions.

Coaching Points:

1. Check for proper stance and set up.

2. Make sure the blocker executes proper punch technique and keeps himself separated from the defender.

3. Check for over extension.

4. Make sure the blocker shuffles his feet quickly and always has a base beneath himself.

Variation: Mirror dodge without helmet.

7 PUSH-PULL DRILL

Purpose: To teach the blocker to maintain balance and fight pressure where he feels pressure.

Execution: Divide the lineman into two groups. Pair them up, and position them on a selected line of scrimmage. One group is designated as the blockers and the other group is designated as the defenders. The first group begins the drill in a lockout position with the defender grabbing the shoulders of the blocker. On the coach's command, the defender attempts to turn the lineman's shoulders, pull the lineman forward or push the lineman back. The lineman must keep his arms locked out and shuffle his feet. The drill continues until coach blows the whistle.

Coaching Points:

1. Make sure the blocker maintains the lockout position throughout the drill.
2. Check for proper body position and footwork.

C

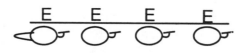

8 REACT AND RECOVER DRILL

Purpose: To develop good foot and hip movement for change of direction.

Execution: Lineman gets into his stance on a selected line of scrimmage with a defender at least two yards outside of him. Position a stand up dummy to represent the quarterback's drop. On the coach's command, the lineman steps back and out with his outside foot and shuffles to a point where he will meet the defender. The lineman will get his outside leg to the crotch of the rusher and punch with the outside hand to the inside number. When contact is made, the rusher will move to the inside as quickly as possible. The lineman will change direction and drive the defender past the dummy without giving ground. The drill should be conducted until all linemen have had a sufficient number of repetitions.

Coaching Points:

1. Check for proper stance and setup. The set should be done as quickly as possible without crossing the feet.

2. Make sure the punch is executed properly and at the correct target.

3. Make sure that there is no wasted motion in the change of direction.

4. Make sure the blocker keeps the defender from the stand up dummy.

7

TIGHT END DRILLS

"Success is to be measured not so much by the position that one has reached in life as by the obstacles which he has overcome while trying to succeed."

— author unknown

The tight end position is a very unique position because it requires blocking *and* receiving skills. During running situations, the tight end has key blocking responsibilities in addition to being the primary receiver in some passing situations. The tight end must be physical enough to be a devastating blocker yet agile enough to be a sure-handed receiver.

STANCE

The tight end's stance should be one which is comfortable, and one that will allow him to execute all his techniques without a loss of balance. The feet should be approximately shoulder width apart, with a toe-to-instep relationship. His weight should be evenly distributed between the balls of the feet and the down-hand. His tail should be raised slightly above parallel to the ground, and his head should be up with his eyes focused on the defense.

THE TIGHT END AS A BLOCKER

The same blocking progression that was presented for the offensive linemen may be taught to the tight ends. The tight ends should be included in most of the offensive line blocking drills with emphasis placed on the same coaching points.

1 COMBINATION BLOCKING DRILL

Purpose: To teach the proper techniques and fundamentals of combination blocking with the tight end and tackle.

Execution: Align the first tight end and tackle on a selected line of scrimmage. Position the defenders in the appropriate alignments. The coach gives the cadence and the designated play. On the snap count, the offensive tackle and tight end execute proper technique in combination blocking scheme. The drill should be conducted on both sides, against a variety of looks, and until all personnel have received a sufficient number of repetitions.

Coaching Points:

1. Check for proper stance and starts. Change up the snap count.

2. Check to see that blockers are executing proper technique.

3. Work every type of scheme against a variety of looks.

2 ARC BLOCK DRILL

Purpose: To teach proper technique in the execution of the arc block.

Execution: Align a defender over the tight end position and a defender five yards outside and five yards deep from the tight end. The coach designates the play, technique, and starting count. On the cadence, the tight end escapes the defensive end and executes an arc block on the support player. The drill should be conducted to both sides and until all tight ends have had a sufficient number of repetitions.

Coaching Points:

1. Check for proper stance.

2. The tight end's escape move should consist of three steps: (1) lateral flat step (2) crossover step and (3) plant step with emphasis on gaining width.

3. The tight end should gather himself under control and attack the outside number of the support player.

4. The tight end cannot allow himself to be defeated underneath. He should force the defender deep and to the inside.

5. When the tight end feels the pursuit and ball carrier getting close, he should now execute a chop block.

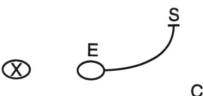

TIGHT END AS A RECEIVER

In order for the tight end to be effective in the passing game, he must be able to release from the line of scrimmage quickly and put pressure on the defensive coverage. The first objective is to beat the man aligned over him without being forced outside his two yard release zone. This can be accomplished in three ways: 1) coming off the ball full speed, 2) executing proper escape technique, and 3) taking the proper line split.

(For more tight end receiving drills, please see the wide receiver drills in the preceding chapter.)

1 RELEASE DRILL

Purpose: To teach tight ends proper release technique.

Execution: Align two bags three yards apart on a selected line of scrimmage. The tight ends align between the bags with a defender. Instruct the defender on what technique to play. The coach designates route and snap count. On the snap count, the tight end executes an escape move and gets into his route. The drill should be conducted from both sides and until all tight ends have received a sufficient number of repetitions.

Coaching Points:

1. Check for proper stance.

2. Check to see that tight end executes proper release (swim, rip, etc.) without being knocked out of his release zone.

3. Change the alignments of the defender (head up, inside shade, or outside shade).

8

GROUP PASS DRILLS

"Coming together is a beginning; keeping together is progress; working together is success"

—Henry Ford

1 SCAN DRILL

Purpose: To develop proper mechanics in dropping and reading the open receiver.

Personnel: Quarterbacks, receivers, and a center.

Execution: Align a quarterback and a center at a designated line of scrimmage in the middle of the field. Position a receiver 10 yards deep on each hash mark. Position a third receiver 10 yards deep directly in front of quarterback. The coach designates the drop, snap count and intended receiver. On the snap, the quarterback executes the proper drop and begins scanning for the open receiver. As the quarterback sets up, the coach points to intended receiver. The intended receiver puts his hands in front of his body, while the other two receivers fold their arms. Reading the signal, the quarterback passes to the designated receiver. The drill should also be run from both hash marks.

Coaching Points:

1. Make sure quarterback-center exchange is executed properly.
2. Check quarterback's drop and throwing mechanics.
3. Make sure quarterback makes proper read and throws an accurate pass.

2 POCKET DRILL

Purpose: To teach the quarterback to get a feel for pocket pass protection against pressure.

Personnel: Quarterbacks, three wide receivers, four offensive linemen, and four defensive linemen.

Execution: Align a quarterback and an offensive lineman on the designated line of scrimmage in the middle of the field. Position the defensive linemen as defensive ends and tackles. Position a receiver 10 yards deep on each hash mark. Position a third receiver 10 yards deep directly in front of quarterback. The coach designates the type of drop (five or seven step), the type of rush (speed or twist), and the intended receiver. The intended receiver will put his hands in front of his body while the other two receivers fold their arms.

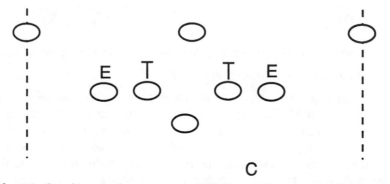

Example #1 On the coaches command: "Five step, speed rush," he will point to the intended receiver.

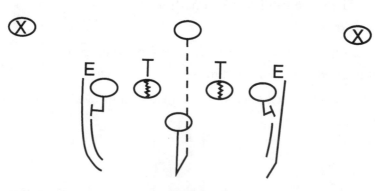

Coaching Points:

1. Check the quarterback's five-step drop technique.
2. The quarterback feels outside pressure, steps up into pocket.
3. Check the quarterback's throwing mechanics.
4. Make sure the quarterback makes proper read and throws an accurate pass.

3 PAT AND GO DRILL

Purpose: To develop proper mechanics in throwing the long ball.

Personnel: Quarterbacks and receivers.

Execution: Align the quarterbacks on the hash marks, one group on the 40-yard line and the other group on the goal line. Divide the receivers and align them on adjacent sideline. On the quarterback's cadence, the wide receiver runs a streak route down near the sideline at ¾ speed. The quarterback proceeds to throw the streak route. After the receiver catches the ball, he returns the football to the quarterback on the other hash mark and changes lines. Both lines are running simultaneously. The drill continues until all quarterbacks have thrown a sufficient number of passes.

Coaching Points:

1. A good drill for developing a high throwing release and putting the proper touch on the long ball.

2. The coach should ensure that the players are using proper mechanics in throwing the football.

Variation: Insert a defensive back in a press alignment trailing the receiver to make the drill more realistic.

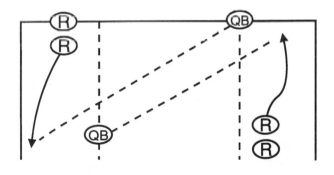

4 QUICK DRILL

Purpose: To develop the proper technique and fundamentals used in the quick game.

Personnel: Quarterbacks and receivers.

Execution: Align two quarterbacks in middle of the field on a selected line of scrimmage. Divide the receivers into two groups aligned near the numbers. The first quarterback works with the receivers to his right, and the second quarterback works with the receivers to his left. The quarterback signals the route (one, two or three route), and the receiver takes the appropriate split. On the snap, the quarterback executes a three-step drop and the receiver runs the designated route. While the first group is executing the drill, the second quarterback signals to the receiver on his side for a specific route.

Coaching Points:

1. The drill should be run full speed — work for repetitions.
2. Make sure the quarterbacks are using proper drop and throwing mechanics.
3. Make sure receivers are executing proper techniques.

Variation: Insert corners in press alignment to work route conversions.

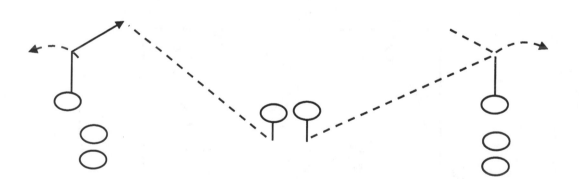

5 THREE-ON-THREE PASS DRILL

Purpose: To develop the proper fundamentals and techniques in various patterns.

Personnel: Quarterbacks, tight ends, and receivers.

Execution: Align three quarterbacks (A,B,C) at a selected line of scrimmage in the middle of the field (four feet apart). Two receivers align to the left. The coach designates the play, for example: "Right 628". Each receiver must be aligned with a proper split relative to the quarterback who will be throwing him the ball and to the pattern to be run. Quarterback "A" is responsible for X receiver, quarterback "B" is responsible for the tight end, and quarterback "C" is responsible for the Z receiver. Quarterback "B" calls the cadence. On the snap, each quarterback executes a seven step drop and the receivers run their designated routes. The drill should be run from both right and left formations and should continue until the quarterbacks and receivers have run a sufficient number of pass plays.

Coaching Points:

1. The drill should be run at full speed — work for repetitions.
2. Make sure quarterbacks are using proper drop and throwing mechanics.
3. Make sure the receivers are executing proper route techniques.
4. Rotate quarterbacks after each pass - A to B, B to C, C to A.
5. Receivers rotate after each reception.

Variation: Incorporate running back position to replace tight end position.

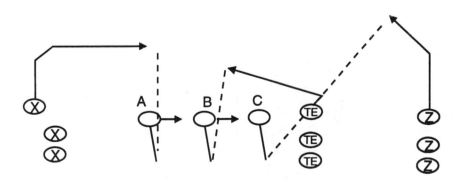

6 HALF LINE PASSING DRILL

Purpose: To teach and practice the proper fundamentals and techniques for reading half-field coverage.

Personnel: Offensive skill positions, center, linebackers, and secondary.

Execution: Divide the offense and the defense into two groups. Align the first offensive group (center, quarterback, running back, tight end, and Z receiver) on a selected line of scrimmage in the middle of the field. Position the defensive unit in a desired coverage. The first offensive unit executes a play, while the second offensive group (quarterback, running back, X and Y receivers), huddles up and calls the next play. The second group executes the play called, while the first group huddles and calls the next play. Receivers alternate after each play within this group. The center snaps for both sides. After a sufficient number of repetitions, the players switch sides and personnel.

Coaching Points:

1. Drill should be run at full speed — no tackling.
2. Emphasis on repetitions: three to four plays per minute.
3. Check for proper quarterback-center exchange.
4. Check quarterback mechanics and proper coverage read.
5. Make sure receivers are executing proper route technique.
6. The defense never huddles, coach signals coverage.

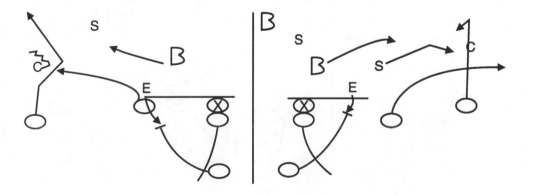

7 INDIVIDUAL CUTS

Purpose: To teach and practice the proper fundamentals in the passing game against man coverage.

Personnel: Quarterbacks, receivers, tight ends and defensive backs.

Execution: Align three quarterbacks (A, B, and C) at a selected line of scrimmage in the middle of the field. Two receivers align to the right, the tight ends align to the right, and the X receivers align to the left. Divide the secondary: left corners on the left, right corners on the right, and safeties with the tight ends. Quarterback "A" works with the X receiver, quarterback "B" works with the tight end, and quarterback "C" works with the Z receiver. Quarterback "A" signals the pass pattern to the X receiver. On the snap, the quarterback and receiver execute proper technique against a defensive back in man coverage. While quarterback "A" and the X receiver are running the drill, quarterback "B" signals the route to the tight end and quarterback "C" signals the route to the Z receiver. After the receiver runs the pattern, he brings the ball back and goes to the end of the line. The quarterbacks rotate after each pass — A to B, B to C, and C to A. The defensive backs rotate after each coverage.

Coaching Points:

1. The drill should be run at full speed — work for repetitions.

2. Make sure quarterbacks are executing proper drop and throwing mechanics.

3. Make sure receivers are executing proper route techniques.

4. Defensive backs execute either a cushion or press technique.

Variation: Use running backs and linebackers.

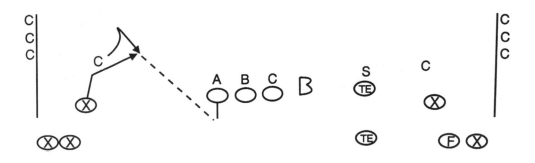

8 SKELETON DRILL

Purpose: To teach and practice the proper fundamentals and techniques for reading defensive coverage.

Personnel: Offensive skill positions, center, linebackers and secondary.

Execution: This drill is scripted both offensively and defensively. Divide the offense into two groups (first team and second team). Group one huddles and calls play one on the offensive script. The first defensive unit huddles and calls play one on the defensive script. Group one breaks their huddle, aligns on a desired line of scrimmage and executes play called. While group one is aligned on the line of scrimmage, group two huddles and calls play two on the offensive script. When the play is over, both the offense and defense units must hustle back. The first defensive group takes 5-10 repetitions and rotates with the second defensive group (scripted). The drill is scripted for 30 plays (10 on each hash mark) and 10 plays in the middle of the field.

Coaching Points:

1. Good pass drill for both offense and defense.

2. If a drill is used as a demonstration drill for an upcoming opponent, coverages or routes may have to be carded.

3. The drill should be run at full speed. Goal is to run two to three plays per minute.

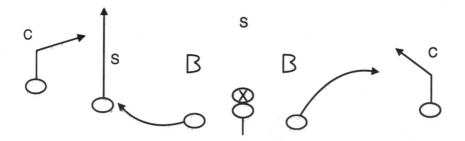

9 ONE-ON-ONE PASS PROTECTION

Purpose: To practice one-on-one pass protection against a defensive line.

Equipment: Paint six 5 × 5 yd. squares on the field.

Execution: Offensive linemen align in their stance on a selected line of scrimmage. The defensive players align opposite the blockers in their regular stance and alignments. Position a stand up dummy to represent the quarterback's drop. On the coach's command, the offensive lineman sets up and pass blocks the defensive player. If the defender runs out or is forced out of the square, the offense wins. If the defenders stay within the square and knock over the stand up dummy, the defense wins. The drill should be conducted so that all linemen receive a sufficient number of repetitions.

Coaching Points:

1. Good competitive drill for both offense and defense.
2. Check for proper pass blocking techniques, pre-snap read, set, punch, body control, and finish.

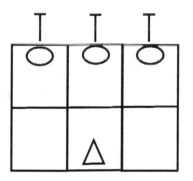

10 FULL LINE PASS RUSH DRILL

Purpose: To teach proper techniques involved in pass rushing and pass blocking.

Personnel: The offensive and defensive lines.

Execution: Pass protection and pass stunts are scripted. Position the first offensive and the first defensive lines on a selected line of scrimmage. Place a stand up dummy seven yards deep representing the quarterback's drop. On the snap, all the defenders will rush utilizing pass rush techniques. The offensive line executes designated pass protection. The drill should be conducted until all personnel receive a sufficient number of repetitions.

Coaching Points:

1. Script stunts against a specific protection as per game plan.
2. Make sure defenders stay in proper pass rush lanes.
3. Check for proper pass rush techniques.
4. Avoid pile ups with the offensive line — quick whistle.

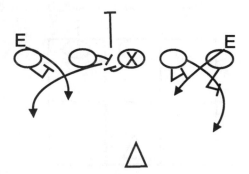

9

GROUP OPTION RUNNING GAME DRILLS

"Regardless of what you do put in, every game boils down to doing the things you do best, and doing them over and over again."

—- author unknown

QUARTERBACK TRIPLE OPTION TECHNIQUES (RIDE AND DECIDE)

Stance

The stance of the quarterback should be one that is comfortable to him. He should have a slight bend in his knees, and a parallel stance with his weight on the balls of his feet. If the quarterback is to front out to the right, he should put pressure on his left toes so that he can pivot and open up without taking a false step. By the same token, if the quarterback is to open up to his left, he should put pressure on his right toes.

First Step

A clock system may be used to teach the quarterback his first direction step in the triple option. If the play calls for the quarterback to front out to the right, he should pivot off his trail foot (left) and open step to five o'clock with his right foot. If the play called requires the quarterback to open up to left, his first step should be at seven o'clock, while pivoting off his right foot. By opening up this deep, the quarterback can get the ball deep to the fullback.

117

Mesh Point (Ride and Decide)

After taking the snap from the center, the quarterback should lock his backside elbow on his hip to get the ball to the fullback's pocket as deep as possible. We refer to this as the swinging gate technique. The quarterback puts his chin on his front side shoulder and his eyes immediately go to the read key.

The quarterback should have a secure grip on the football when he gets to the mesh point. It is helpful to teach the quarterback to use the back of his inside hand as a pressure gauge for the fullback. The quarterback will ride only to the front hip of the fullback and not beyond. The quarterback should not ride past this point because it is after that point that most turnovers occur. If the quarterback gives the ball off, he simply removes the inside hand from the fullback's hips and carries out the fake. If he disconnects on the fullback, he uses both hands to remove the ball from the fullback's pocket and continues to pitch key.

The Read

Teach the quarterback to read the shoulders of the read key. If the read key's shoulders are turned, coming flat towards the fullback's track, the quarterback should disconnect on the fullback and attack the pitch key. If the read key's shoulders are upfield or coming toward the quarterback, give the ball to the fullback, If there is any indecision on the type of charge by the read key, give the fullback the ball. It is the quarterback's decision whether or not to give the ball to the fullback.

The Fullback's Course

The fullback's alignment is four yards deep and directly behind the quarterback. On the snap, the fullback sprints on a course to the outside shoulder of the guard. The fullback should take a six inch lead step with the first step to get on the right track. The fullback will not come off this track until after he hits the mesh point. It's important that the fullback give the quarterback an open pocket by raising his inside arm. The fullback should feel the pressure of the quarterback's hands to indicate whether he's giving him the ball or disconnecting it.

Pitch Key - Eliminate!

After disengaging on the fullback, it is imperative to attack the pitch key and force him to commit to either the quarterback or pitch. We teach the quarterback to sprint to the pitch key's inside shoulder. If the pitch key widens or works up field, the quarterback should cut up inside and be alert for the alley player. If the pitch key comes for the quarterback, he should pitch the ball to the trail back. The most important coaching point is to make the pitch key commit to his responsibility as quickly as possible. Teams run into problems when they allow the pitch key to slow play the quarterback's decision and string out the play which permits the opponent to run it down.

1   V-DRILL

Purpose: To teach and develop proper mechanics in executing the first phase of the triple option-mesh point.

Personnel: Quarterbacks, centers and fullbacks.

Execution: Align personnel in appropriate alignments. The coach designates the direction of the play (for example: six option right). On the snap, the quarterback executes the proper mechanics in the ride and decide. The fullback takes a six inch lead step and sprints to the outside shoulder of guard (down the line). The quarterback gives the ball to the fullback and carries out the option fake. The drill should be run both to the right and the left. The drill continues until all personnel have had a sufficient number of repetitions.

Coaching Points:

1. Check for proper center-quarterback exchange.
2. Make sure quarterbacks are executing proper footwork. First step should be at five or seven o'clock. (No false steps.)
3. Check fullback's course.
4. Pay particular attention to mesh point — quarterback reaching the ball deep, fullback pocket, quarterback's hands and eyes, fullback clamping both arms over ball. Repetitions are key to this drill; they allow quarterback and fullback to get a feel for the ride and decide phase of triple option.

Variation: Coach aligns as handoff key.

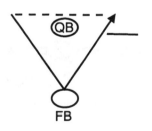

2 RIDE AND DECIDE DRILL

Purpose: To teach and practice proper fundamentals in reading the handoff key.

Equipment: Line spacing strip

Personnel: Quarterbacks, center, fullbacks, and defensive ends.

Execution: Align personnel in appropriate positions. The coach designates the play and the handoff keys responsibility. On the snap, the quarterback and fullback execute proper mechanics in the ride and decide. The quarterback reads the handoff key and reacts accordingly. The drill should be conducted to both the right and left and continues until quarterbacks and fullbacks have had a sufficient number of repetitions.

Coaching Points:

1. Make sure quarterback-center exchange is executed properly.
2. Check quarterback's footwork.
3. Make sure quarterback and fullback have proper course (track).
4. Instruct quarterback not to ride fullback past his front hip.
5. Make sure quarterback makes proper read.
6. Change up handoff keys technique to give quarterback different looks.
7. No turnovers — ball security is key.

Variation: Insert a halfback into the drill. If the quarterback gives the ball to the fullback, the coach immediately tosses the quarterback the ball he is holding. The coach now becomes the pitch key. The quarterback reads the coach and either cuts upfield or pitches the ball to the halfback.

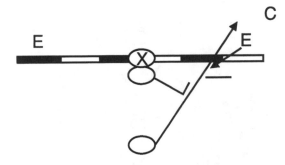

3 PITCH DRILL

Purpose: To teach and develop proper fundamentals in pitching the football.

Execution: The drill is set up with two quarterbacks standing on the sideline at a five-yard interval. The quarterback with the ball jogs in place ready to pitch the ball. The other quarterback begins running down his respective yard line working to get in a proper pitch phase. The quarterback with the ball takes off and executes the pitch. As the quarterback receives the pitch, he begins to jog while the other quarterback works to get into pitch phase. The drill continues all the way across the field, the players then turn around and come back the same way. The drill should be conducted so both quarterbacks work the right- and left-hand pitch. Repeat a predetermined number of times.

Coaching Point: Make sure quarterbacks execute proper pitch technique.

Variation: May also be used as a running back drill.

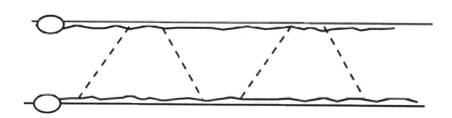

4 TRIPLE OPTION DRILL

Purpose: To teach and practice the proper techniques and fundamentals in executing the triple option play.

Personnel: Offensive backfield, center, and backup defenders.

Execution: Place a line strip at a selected line of scrimmage in the middle of the field. Divide offense into two groups. Align two defenders (handoff keys) over the offensive tackle position and two defenders (pitch keys) in designated alignments. The offensive backfield aligns accordingly. The coach instructs the handoff and pitch keys as to their responsibilities. The coach calls the play, (for example, "6 option".) On the snap, the first offense group executes proper fundamentals and techniques. The second group huddles, calls the next play and executes option when the first group finishes. The drill should also be conducted from both the right and left hash marks. The drill continues until all groups run a sufficient number of repetitions.

Coaching Points:

1. The drill should be run full speed — repetitions are key.

2. Make sure the quarterback-center exchange is executed properly.

3. Make sure handoff and pitch keys are executing proper responsibilities.

4. Check to see that offensive backfield is executing proper fundamentals and techniques.

5. Change up looks and charges according to game plan.

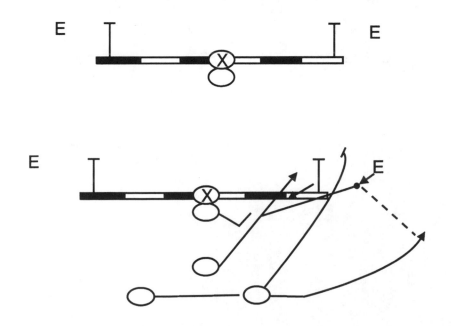

5 HALF LINE OPTION DRILL

Purpose: To teach and develop proper technique and fundamentals in the execution of triple option.

Personnel: Offense and scout defense.

Execution: Offensive and defensive plays are scripted (20 plays: 10 right hash boundary and field, and 10 left hash boundary and field.) Divide offense into two groups: quarterback, back field, tight end, and receiver on each side of the line. Align the ball on a selected line of scrimmage on the left hashmark. Most coaching in this drill is done by getting the defense lined up with proper assignments. The first group huddles, calls the first play on script, and hustles up to the line of scrimmage (play calls for tight end or wide receiver, possibly both). While the first group executes a play into the boundary, the second group huddles and calls play two to be run to the field. It's important that both groups hustle back to huddle after the play — repetitions are key to this drill. The drill should be conducted from both hash marks. The drill should continue until both groups get a significant number of repetitions (depending on script).

Coaching Points:

1. The drill should be conducted at full speed. (Work to get two or three repetitions per minute.)

2. Make sure offensive personnel are executing proper techniques and fundamentals.

3. Make sure defensive personnel are aligned correctly and playing their proper assignments.

4. Script triple option plays against defenses as per game plan.

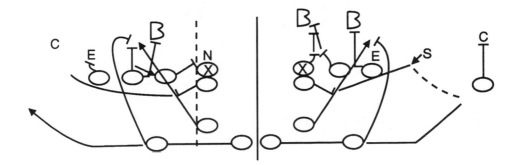

6 HALF LINE DRILL

Purpose: To practice proper fundamentals both offensively and defensively in a half line situation.

Personnel: Offense and scout defense.

Execution: Offensive and defensive plays are scripted (20 plays: 10 right hash boundary and field and 10 left hash boundary and field.) Divide offense and defense into two groups. Align the football on a selected line of scrimmage on the left hashmark. Boundary personnel (group one) steps up and executes play number one on the script. Field personnel (group two) huddles, calls play number two on the script and executes the play as group one finishes. The drill should be run from both hash marks and until all personnel have had a sufficient number of repetitions.

Coaching Points:

1. Check for proper stances and alignments.

2. Make sure all personnel use proper techniques and fundamentals of running, passing, blocking, receiving, attacking, shedding blocks and tackling.

3. Work for quality repetitions.

7 NINE-ON-SEVEN

Purpose: To practice proper fundamentals both offensively and defensively in a full line situation.

Personnel: Offense and defense.

Execution: Offense and defensive plays are scripted (20-30 plays). Divide both offense and defense into first and second units. Secondary and receivers are not included. Align the football on a selected line of scrimmage. The first offensive unit huddles, calls play one on the script and hustles up to the line of scrimmage. As the first offensive unit is on the line, the second offensive unit huddles and calls play two on the script. The first defensive unit runs six consecutive plays then rotates with the second defensive unit, which runs four consecutive plays. The drill should be conducted until all personnel have had a sufficient number of repetitions.

Coaching Points:

1. Check for proper stances and alignments.

2. Set the tempo for the drill (for example, ¾ speed, full speed).

3. Make sure all personnel use proper techniques and fundamentals of running, blocking, attacking, shedding blocks and tackling.

4. Work for quality repetitions.

Variations: Situation scrimmages: goal line scrimmage, red zone scrimmage, coming out scrimmage, short yardage scrimmage, or long yardage scrimmage.

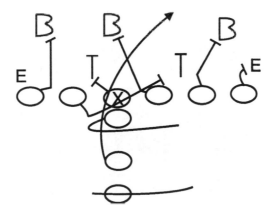

10

PURSUIT AND TACKLING DRILLS

"The race is not always to the swift, but to the one who keeps on running"

—author unknown

"Some of us will do our jobs well and some will not, but we will all be judged by one thing: the result."

—author unknown

PURSUIT

In order to be a great defensive player, the player must have great pursuit on each and every play. Effective pursuit is the result of great desire and motivation. It results in big plays for the defense, eliminates big plays for the offense and overcomes individual defensive mistakes. Pursuit must be practiced in every drill to develop the intensity necessary to be successful.

1   PURSUIT DRILL

Purpose: To teach defensive personnel proper pursuit angles. To provide an overall conditioning drill.

Execution: The defense huddles on a selected line of scrimmage. Align two cones, one on each side of the field on top of the numbers. Position a running back on each hashmark, five yards behind the selected line of scrimmage. The coach calls out the defensive play. The defense lines up accordingly in proper stance and alignments. On the cadence, the coach either drops straight back and throws the ball deep or turns and simulates a toss sweep. If the coach drops straight back, the defensive line rushes and the secondary and linebackers drop to their respective zones. The coach throws the ball deep, and the defender intercepts the football at its highest point and returns it up the near sideline. The remaining defenders set up a wall leading the ball carrier into the end zone. If the coach simulates a toss sweep, the ball carrier on the hashmark sprints around the cone and down the sideline. The drill may be run to simulate a drive in a hurry-hurry situation.

Coaching Points:

1. Make sure all defenders sprint in their proper pursuit angles.

2. Instruct the defenders to be in position to make the play but not touch the ball carrier.

3. Coaches must be very demanding of their players' effort to get to the football.

Variations:

- 8-10 play drive
- Work sudden change situation after an 8-10 play drive

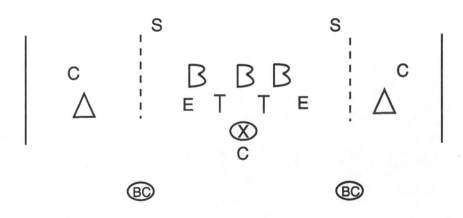

TACKLING

A tackle is a desired collision between the defensive man and the ball carrier in which the defensive man must win. Tackling is the most important phase of defense. A defender may be able to execute all other phases of defense correctly, but if he cannot tackle, he cannot play.

Players must know and understand the proper way to tackle in order to play effectively and safely. The number one reason to use proper technique is for safety purposes. Defenders should never lower their heads and make contact with the top of their helmets. Defenders who choose to disregard this rule are subjecting themselves and others to severe head and neck injuries.

Proper technique also makes the defenders good tacklers and qualifies them to play. Tackling is best taught in three phases: approach, contact, and follow through.

Approach

The most important phase of the approach is that the defender must position himself so that he allows the ball carrier only one way to go. If the defender gets himself into a head up position, the ball carrier has three ways to go, making the tackle that much more difficult. We teach our defensive players to keep their momentum under control until they get within three to four yards of the ball carrier. They should break down in a good hitting position with a good base, short choppy steps while closing the distance on the ball carrier.

Contact

The pop is the coordinated skill of making contact in the correct position while rolling the hips, thrusting the arms and utilizing the power of the lower back and legs. The first contact is made with the chest or shoulders. The arms are utilized in three steps:

1. As contact is made, the arms are thrust in an upward direction around the ball carrier.

2. The arms are then wrapped around the buttocks of the ball carrier.

3. Finally, the arms are used to pull the ball carrier towards the defender.

Follow Through

The combination of the contact and the leg drive allows the defender to finish the tackle by placing the ball carrier on his back.

1 FIT POSITION

Purpose: To teach the defenders the ideal tackling (fit) position.

Execution: Divide the defenders into two groups and align them on a selected line of scrimmage. Designate one group as the defenders and the other as the ball carriers. On the coach's command, the defenders will walk up into the fit position. The defender should hold the position until he has been critiqued by the coach. The drill should continue until all defenders have worked both the right and left side fit positions.

Coaching Points:

1. Check to see that the defender has a proper base. The knees should be bent, feet approximately shoulder width apart with power producing angles in the legs.

2. The butt should be out, the back should be flat and the arms should be wrapped around the buttocks.

3. Contact should be made with the front of the shoulder or chest; the head should be up, neck bowed and eyes open.

2 FIT AND LIFT

Purpose: To teach the defenders the ideal tackling position with emphasis on the follow through phase of the tackle.

Execution: Divide the defenders into two groups and align them on a selected line of scrimmage. Designate one group as the defenders and the other as the ball carriers. On the coach's first command, the defender walks up into the fit position. On the coach's second command, the defenders roll their hips and explode up and through the ball carriers, taking them back five yards. The drill is repeated until all defenders have worked a right and left shoulder fit and lift.

Coaching Points:

1. Align the defender's feet on a selected line of scrimmage. The coach should stand on one side of the players so he can see the hip roll.

2. Instruct the ball carriers to assist the defender by jumping up in the air on the second coach's command.

3. The drill's emphasis should be on leverage.

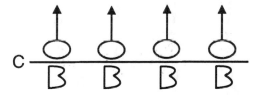

3 FORM TACKLE

Purpose: To teach proper techniques and fundamentals in tackling.

Execution: Divide the defenders into two groups five yards apart facing each other. Designate one group as the defenders and the other group as the ball carriers. On the coach's command, the first ball carrier in line begins jogging towards the defender. The defender steps up and executes a form tackle. The drill continues right down the line and until all defenders have executed a form tackle.

Coaching Points:

1. Check for proper approach.

2. Make sure the defender executes proper tackling techniques.

3. Instruct the ball carriers not to give any resistance on contact.

4 POPSICLE TACKLING DRILL

Purpose: To teach proper techniques and fundamentals involved in tackling.

Equipment: One man sled (popsicle)

Execution: Align the defenders in a single file line five yards apart from the popsicle sled. On the coach's command, the first defender executes a proper form tackle on the sled. After each repetition, each defender goes to the end of the line. The drill continues until all defenders have executed form tackles with both the right and left shoulders.

Coaching Points:

1. Check for proper approach, contact, and follow through.

2. Emphasize attacking the sled with leverage and rolling the hips on contact.

3. The follow through phase of the tackle cannot be accomplished until the sled is driven off the ground.

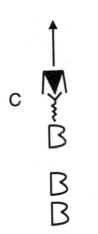

5 GOAL LINE TACKLE DRILL

Purpose: To teach proper technique and fundamentals in tackling.

Execution: Divide the defenders into two groups and designate one group as the defenders and the other as the ball carriers. Align two cones on a selected line of scrimmage five yards apart. Position the defender with his heels on the line of scrimmage and the ball carrier three yards away. On the cadence, the ball carrier tries to run between the cones and score. The defender steps up and executes a tackle. The drill should be conducted until all defenders have had a sufficient number or repetitions.

Coaching Points:

1. Run the drill at full speed. Instruct the ball carrier to try anything that will enable him to cross the goal line.

2. Check for proper tackling technique.

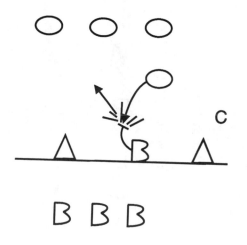

6 EYE OPENER

Purpose: To combine tackling skills with proper pursuit leverage and position.

Equipment: Four to six tackling dummies/bags.

Execution: Position four to six dummies two yards apart. Divide the defenders into two groups facing each other and designate one group as the ball carriers and one as the defenders. The ball carriers will stand approximately a ½ yard closer to the bag. The coach stands behind the defender line and signals which hole the ball carrier should run through. On the coach's cadence, the ball carrier and the defender run parallel to the dummies. When the ball carrier turns into the designated hole, the defender steps up and executes proper tackling techniques. The drill continues in both directions and until all defenders have had a sufficient number of repetitions.

Coaching Points:

1. The drill may be conducted at half to full speed.

2. Emphasize staying on the backside of the ball carrier and never over running the cutback.

3. Check for proper tackling technique.

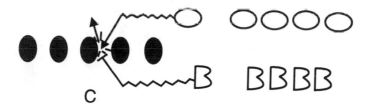

7 ANGLE TACKLE

Purpose: To combine tackling skills with proper pursuit leverage and position.

Execution: Align two cones five yards apart. Divide defenders into two single file lines five yards apart facing one another and designate one group as the ball carriers and the other group as the defenders. The coach stands behind the first defender and signals the direction to the ball carrier. On the coach's cadence, the ball carrier takes off to the designated cone. The defender closes the distance and executes a proper angle tackle. The drill should be conducted so that all defenders work angle tackling to both the right and left sides.

Coaching Points:

1. The drill may be conducted at half to full speed.
2. Emphasize staying on the backside of the ball carrier and never over running the cutback.
3. The defender should work to get his head across the ball carrier's body on contact.
4. Check for proper tackling technique.

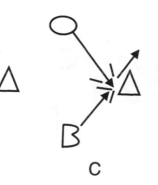

8 BUTT DRILL

Purpose: To teach proper tackling techniques.

Equipment: Four dummies and one cone.

Execution: Position four dummies two yards apart and place a cone five yards after the fourth bag. Divide the defenders into two groups and designate one group as the ball carriers and the other as the defenders. On command, one ball carrier and one defender begin shuffling to the first bag. As the ball carrier enters the first chute, the defender will butt the ball carrier by hitting on the backside shoulder, rolling hips and wrapping with the arms. At this point, the defender releases the ball carrier, backpedals, shuffles and attacks the ball carrier in the second chute. The drill continues through the third chute. After the ball carrier is released, he should backpedal and run to the cone. The defender should execute an angle tackle as the ball carrier runs to the cone. The drill should be conducted in both directions and until all defenders have had a sufficient number of repetitions.

Coaching Points:

1. Make sure defender attacks with inside out leverage.

2. Emphasize hip roll and arm wrap on contact.

3. Check for proper angle tackle technique.

4. This is a good drill for defenders to work to regain their base after contact.

9 OPEN FIELD TACKLING

Purpose: To teach the defender to break down in open field and make open field tackle.

Equipment: Three dummies (bags) and four cones.

Execution: Lay three bags together with a cone five yards outside either edge. Position two cones three to four yards apart directly in the middle of the bags. Divide the defenders into two groups and designate one group as the ball carriers and the other as the defenders. On the coach's command, the ball carrier should run to the middle cone and break off in either direction between the bag and the cone. The defender should close the distance on the ball carrier and execute an open field tackle. The drill should continue until all defenders have had a sufficient number of repetitions.

Coaching Points:

1. The drill's emphasis should be on closing the distance on the ball carrier and gathering momentum under control.

2. As the ball carrier commits to a side, the defender should keep the inside-out relationship to nullify the cutback.

3. Make sure the defender executes proper tackling technique.

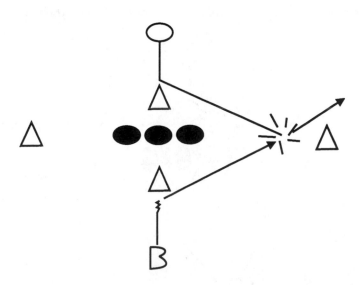

10 SIDELINE TACKLING DRILL

Purpose: To teach defenders to keep proper leverage on the ball carrier by using the sideline to their advantage.

Equipment: Three cones.

Execution: Align one cone inside the hashmark and one cone outside the hashmark 15 to 20 yards apart. Position a third cone between the other two on top of the numbers. Divide the defenders into two groups and position the designated defensive group behind the first cone and the designated ball carrier group behind the second cone. On the coach's command, the ball carrier will run to the middle cone and attempt to run by the defender. The defender will close the distance on the ball carrier and execute an angle tackle using the sideline as a twelfth defender. The drill should be conducted in both directions and until all defenders have had a sufficient number of repetitions.

Coaching Points:

1. Instruct the ball carrier to feel where the defender is located. If the defender over runs the ball carrier, instruct him to cut back. If the defender stays back side, attempt to beat him down the sideline.

2. The defender should work to stay on the backside hip of the ball carrier, "pin the man to the sideline."

3. Check to see that the defender breaks down under control and continues to close the distance on the ball carrier.

4. Make sure the defender executes proper tackling technique.

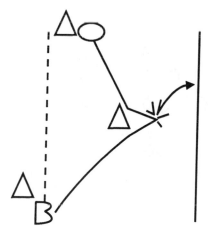

CREATE TURNOVERS

Nothing demoralizes an offense quicker than turnovers. Defensive personnel must be constantly coached to create a turnover whenever given the opportunity. It is a good idea to set aside 10 minutes every day in practice to work turnovers by rotating personnel through four stations.

1 STRIP DRILL

Purpose: To teach secondary players and linebackers to strip the ball from the intended receiver.

Execution: Divide the defenders into two groups and align them five yards apart on the sideline. The coach designates one group as the defenders and one group as the intended receivers. The defender group should move out one yard from the sideline. The coach stands approximately 10 yards from the receiver group on top of the numbers. On the cadence, the receiver runs down the yardline. The defender drives to the interception point. The coach throws the football to the receiver, and the defender executes proper strip technique. The drill should be conducted in both directions and until all defenders have had a sufficient number of repetitions.

Coaching Points:

1. Instruct defenders to drive to the interception point and strip with the outside arm down on the receiver's upfield arm.

2. The coach should throw the ball out and in front of the intended receiver.

3. The defender must work to rip the ball out of the receiver's hands.

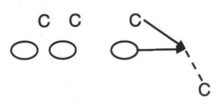

2 FUMBLE TACKLE

Purpose: To develop proper fundamentals of tackling with an emphasis on creating a turnover.

Execution: Divide the defenders into two groups aligned five yards from each other. Designate one group as the ball carriers and the other as the defenders. Instruct the defender to lay on his back with his hips on the line and his head facing the ball carrier. The ball carrier faces away from the defender with his heels on the line, and the ball placed behind his feet. On the cadence, the defender springs to his feet and attacks the ball carrier. The ball carrier turns around, picks up the ball and starts forward toward the defender. The defender aims for the ball, executes a form tackle to create a fumble and scrambles to recover the football. The drill should be conducted so that all personnel receive a sufficient number of repetitions.

Coaching Points:

1. Instruct the ball carrier to release the football as contact is made.

2. The defender should work to put his face on the football and execute proper tackling technique.

3. Make sure defender recovers the football with two hands and cradles his body around the football.

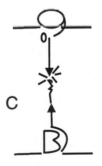

3 SECOND MAN STRIP

Purpose: To teach the second defender to strip the football as the ball carrier has been fronted up by the first defender.

Execution: Divide defenders into three groups. Designate one group as the ball carriers, one group as the tacklers, and the third group as the strippers. This drill uses the same set up as the angle tackle drill. Position the third group five yards away from the cone on the same line as the tackling group. Instruct the ball carrier to carry the football with his outside arm. On the cadence, the ball carrier runs to the cone and the defender executes an angle tackle. When contact has been made, the stripper attacks the ball carrier and rips the ball out of his hands. Rotate personnel after each repetition and conduct the drill until everyone has received a sufficient number of repetitions.

Coaching Points:

1. Make sure the defender executes the proper angle tackle techniques.

2. Instruct the second defender (stripper) to rip the football out of the ball carriers hands and advance the ball upfield.

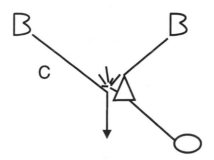

4 CHASE DRILL

Purpose: To teach defenders to strip the football when trailing the ball carrier.

Execution: Divide defenders into two groups and designate one as the ball carriers and the other as the defenders. Align the ball carrier group on a selected line of scrimmage and position the defender group two yards behind them. On the cadence, instruct the first ball carrier to run at half to three-quarter speed straight down the field. The defender sprints to catch up and works to strip the ball from behind. The drill should be conducted in both directions and until all personnel have received a sufficient number of repetitions.

Coaching Points:

1. The number one goal when trailing the ball carrier is to make the tackle. As the defender makes contact with the ball carrier, he should either strip down on the ball or punch up and through the football creating a turnover.

2. As the football is fumbled, the defender should execute proper fumble recovery technique.

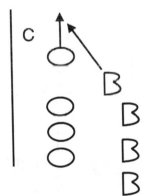

5 OKLAHOMA DRILL

Purpose: To teach defenders to defeat and shed the blockers, and make the tackle on the ball carrier.

Personnel: Both offense and defensive personnel.

Execution: Set up three stations with bags three yards apart on a selected line of scrimmage. Make sure there is plenty of room between each station. Divide personnel accordingly in each station (i.e.: nose guards and linebackers against centers; guards, defensive tackle and defensive ends against tackles and tight ends; defensive backs against wide receivers). Each station will have one quarterback and one running back. Offensive coach designates snap count. On the cadence, the blocker executes a base block and the quarterback hands the ball off to the running back. The running back attempts to run between the bags. The drill continues until all personnel receive a sufficient number of repetitions.

Coaching Points:

1. This is a good competitive drill between the offense and defense. Keep score on how many times the offense was successful in scoring and the defense was successful in stopping them.

2. The quarterback begins the drill with the ball in his hands.

3. Check to see that the defender attacks with leverage and plays with his hands.

4. Make sure the ball carrier runs in between the bags.

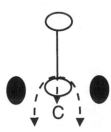 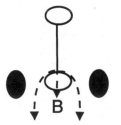 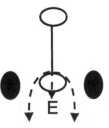

6 FOUR-ON-FOUR DRILL

Purpose: To teach the basic fundamentals of football.

Personnel: Both offensive and defensive personnel.

Execution: Align three offensive linemen on a selected line of scrimmage. Position a wide receiver 10 yards downfield and a quarterback and one running back in the backfield. Position three defenders (defensive line or linebackers) over the offensive linemen. Align a defensive back five yards in front of the wide receiver. The drill should be set up to be 10 yards wide. The offense huddles, calls dive right or dive left, the snap count, and breaks out of the huddle. On the cadence, (quarterback holds ball) the offense executes a dive play with the receiver stalk blocking the defensive back. The defense attacks, sheds blocks and attempts to tackle the ball carrier. The drill continues until all personnel have received a sufficient number of repetitions.

Coaching Points:

1. Good competitive drill between the offense and the defense.
2. All personnel should be instructed to execute proper technique.

7 KENTUCKY GAUNTLET

Purpose: To teach proper tackling in a condensed area.

Execution: Position three lines of tacklers five yards apart facing the running back line. Place markers (jerseys or cones) in five yard intervals forming the boundary. The first man in line steps up. On the cadence, the running back attempts to run by the first defender with only one move. The defender steps up and executes a full speed tackle. The running back gets back on his feet and continues the drill through the third line. The drill is divided up into three stations, one for defensive backs, one for linebackers and one for defensive linemen. All running backs, receivers and tight ends are used as the ball carrier. The drill should continue until all personnel have had a sufficient number of repetitions.

Coaching Points:

1. Good competitive drill between offense and defense.

2. Check to see that all defenders are executing proper tackling form.

3. Check to see that all ball carriers are executing proper ball handling skills.

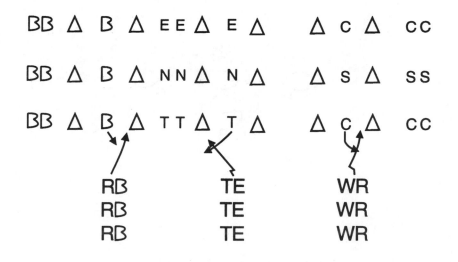

11
DEFENSIVE LINE DRILLS

"It is no disgrace to fail, but to lie there and grunt is."

— author unknown

DEFENSIVE LINE TECHNIQUES

Defensive line play can be categorized into three different techniques:

1. Reading
2. Angle/slant
3. Attacking

Regardless of the technique or front, the base essentials of defensive line play are the same. The defensive lineman must have the ability to play with leverage, to shed blockers, and to get to the football to be successful.

STANCE

The defensive lineman's stance should be one which is feasible for the technique he is playing. The key factor in each stance is weight distribution. For instance, reading and movement fronts would require a more balanced stance, while an attacking front would require an elongated stance.

Balanced Stance

1. The player assumes a three- or four-point stance.
2. The feet should be shoulder width apart with a toe to instep relationship. Toes are pointed straight ahead.
3. The weight is on the balls of the feet with a little air under the heels.
4. The head is in a natural extension, with the back flat and the tail end raised slightly.

Attack Stance

1. The player is in a three-point stance (sprinters stance).
2. The feet should be shoulder width apart with at least a heel to toe relationship. Toes are pointed straight ahead.
3. The weight distribution is forward, with 60% of the weight on the down hand and the up foot.
4. The head is in a natural extension, with a flat back, the tail end slightly raised, and the knees bent ready to recoil.

Two-Point Stance (Defensive Ends/Outside Linebackers)

1. The feet should be no wider than shoulder width apart, in a parallel stance with the weight distributed on the balls of the feet.
2. There should be a good bend in the ankles, knees, and hips.
3. The shoulders should be over the knees with the arms in position to deliver a blow on the tight end.
4. The hands should be out with the thumbs up and the palms close together.

1 STANCE DRILL

Purpose: To teach proper defensive line stance.

Execution: Align the defensive linemen on a selected line of scrimmage. On the coach's command, the defensive linemen get into proper stances. The coach critiques each player's stance. The players should work both right and left handed, two-point and/or four-point stances.

Coaching Points:

1. The feet should be pointed straight ahead, approximately shoulder width apart.
2. The head is in a natural extension, with the back flat and the tail end slightly raised.

TAKE-OFF

The take-off is the initial movement of the defensive lineman triggered by a specific key. Defensive linemen are generally taught to key either the football or the man they are aligned over to begin their initial movement. Regardless of the key, the defensive lineman must take-off on the snap as quickly as possible and attack the blocker with proper leverage.

1 BALL TAKE-OFF DRILL

Purpose: To teach defensive linemen to key the football for take-off.

Execution: Position two or three defensive linemen on a selected line of scrimmage in proper stances. The coach has an old football with a rope tied to it and stands on the other side of the line of scrimmage. The coach calls out signals attempting to draw the defenders offside. When the ball moves, the players explode across the line of scrimmage and the next group gets ready to go. The drill should be conducted until all players receive a sufficient number of repetitions.

Coaching Points:

1. Check for proper stance and take-off technique.

2. Emphasize that the player should take off when the ball does and not on the cadence.

3. Have the players sprint five yards past the line of scrimmage and then hurry to the end of the line.

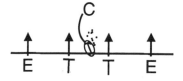

2 MAN TAKE-OFF DRILL

Purpose: To teach defensive linemen to take off and react on the blocker's movement.

Execution: The players pair up, with one player designated as offense and the other as defense. The first paired group aligns on a selected line of scrimmage. The coach begins the drill by calling the cadence. The offensive man moves when he is ready and attempts various blocks. The defender moves on movement, delivers a blow, and reacts accordingly. The drill should be conducted so that all defensive linemen receive a sufficient number of repetitions.

Coaching Points:

1. Check for proper stance and take-off technique.
2. Emphasis should be on the man, not on cadence.
3. Check for proper reaction against a blocking scheme.

EXPLOSION DRILLS

The one-man sled is a device that can be utilized to develop the skills that enable the defensive lineman to deliver an explosive blow with proper leverage. These skills coordinate all body parts into a fluid but explosive movement.

1 SIX POINT DRILL

Purpose: To teach defensive linemen to roll their hips.

Equipment: One-man sled.

Execution: Position the defensive linemen in a single file line directly in front of the one-man sled. The first player in line kneels on all fours in front of and as close to the sled as possible. On the coach's command, the defensive lineman explodes into the sled with proper hand placement and hip roll. The defender gets back on his knees in position to execute the drill again. The drill should be conducted so that all defensive linemen receive a sufficient number of repetitions.

Coaching Points:

1. The defender's knees should stay on the ground. The power should come from the hand explosion and hip roll.

2. Coach the defender to keep his head up.

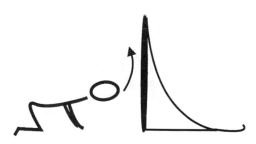 

2 FIVE POINT CONTACT

Purpose: To teach defensive lineman to roll their hips with good power angles in their knees.

Equipment: One-man sled.

Execution: Position the defensive linemen in a single file line directly in front of the one-man sled. The first player in line should kneel down on one knee in front of and as close to the sled as possible. On the coach's command, the defensive lineman explodes into the sled with proper hand placement and hip roll. The defender gets back on his knee and in position to execute the drill again. The lineman should execute the drill driving off both the right and left foot. The drill should be conducted until all defensive linemen receive a sufficient number of repetitions.

Coaching Points:

1. Check to see that the hips sink and roll forward.
2. Check for proper hand placement.
3. Head should be up and out of the contact.

3   TWO, THREE, OR FOUR POINT EXPLOSION

Purpose: To teach defensive linemen to explode out of their stance with proper leverage and defeat the blocker.

Equipment: One-man sled.

Execution: Align defensive linemen in a single file line directly in front of the blocking sled. The first man in line positions himself in appropriate stance one yard away from the sled. Place two cones 10 yards on either side of the sled. On the coach's command, the defender explodes out of his stance and into the sled. The defensive lineman should drive the sled up and continue to chop his feet. On the coach's second command, the defender sheds the blocking sled and sprints to the designated cone. The drill should be conducted until all defensive linemen have had a sufficient number of repetitions.

Coaching Points:

1. Check for proper stance and take-off technique.
2. Make sure defender has proper hand placement and works for separation on the sled.
3. Check for hip roll. The defender should be hitting up and through the sled.
4. On the second command, the defender should shed the blocker and sprint to the designated cone.

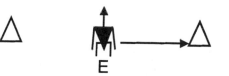

HANDS

When contact is made, the defender must have the ability to play with his hands and play with leverage. The only advantage the rules provide for the defensive players is that they are permitted to use their hands. The hands are necessary to ward off blockers and get to the point of attack against a run or a pass.

1 FIVE-MAN SLED

Purpose: To develop hand explosion, footwork and block protection.

Equipment: Five-man sled.

Execution: Position defensive linemen in a single file line on one side of the sled. The first defensive lineman aligns in his proper stance facing the first dummy. On the coach's cadence, the defender explodes into the dummy with proper leverage and hand position. The defender then sheds the dummy and shuffles down the line and hand shivers the remaining dummies. The drill should be executed in both directions and until all defenders have had a sufficient number of repetitions.

Coaching Points:

1. Check for proper stance.

2. The emphasis should be on quick feet, hand explosion, and disengaging the blocker.

3. Make sure the defenders stay low and attack with leverage.

2 SHED DRILL

Purpose: To teach defensive linemen proper fundamentals in using the hands to defeat blockers.

Execution: Divide defensive linemen into two groups and align them on a selected line of scrimmage facing each other. Designate one line as offense and the other line as defense. On the coach's cadence, the offensive player attempts to drive his helmet past the defenders' left side and knock him off the line of scrimmage. The defender reacts to the block by shuffling to his left and driving his hands into the opponent's numbers. After the defender works to a lockout position, he should work to escape the blocker. The drill should be conducted in both directions and until all defenders have had a sufficient number of repetitions.

Coaching Points:

1. Check for proper stances.
2. Make sure defenders attack with leverage and proper hand placement.
3. Make sure defenders move feet quickly to keep proper body positioning
4. The defenders should work to a lockout position before shedding the block.

3 ONE-ON-ONE BLOCKS

Purpose: To teach defensive linemen proper techniques and fundamentals in defeating blocking schemes.

Execution: Divide defensive linemen into two groups on a selected line of scrimmage. Designate one group as offense and the other as the defensive group. The coach dictates the blocking scheme. On the designated take-off key (ball or man), the defender attacks the blocker and executes the proper technique according to a blocking scheme. The drill should be conducted against a variety of blocking schemes and until all defenders have had a sufficient number of repetitions.

Coaching Points:

1. The drill should be conducted against a variety of blocking schemes, for example: a) base block; b) reach block; c) cut off block; d) pull; and e) pass set.

2. Make sure the defender executes proper technique against a designated block.

4　TWO-ON-ONE BLOCKING SCHEMES

Purpose: To teach defensive lineman proper techniques and fundamentals in defeating blocking schemes.

Execution: Divide defensive linemen into groups of three and designate one player as the defender and the other two as the blockers. The coach dictates the blocking schemes. On a designated take-off key, the defender attacks and executes proper technique according to the blocking scheme. The drill should be conducted against a variety of blocking schemes and until all defenders have had a sufficient number of repetitions.

Coaching Points:

1. The drill should be conducted against a variety of blocking schemes, for example: a) double team; b) reach block; c) cut off; d) pull; and e) pass set.

2. Make sure the defender executes proper technique against a designated block. (See also Half Line and Nine-on-Seven Drills.)

5 CONTAIN DRILL

Purpose: To teach proper position and technique to keep contain responsibilities.

Execution: This drill is run with three players: two blockers and a running back. Align the two blockers behind one another facing the defender. The third man is positioned as a running back and stacked inside against the two blockers. The defender aligns himself head up over the first blocker. On the coach's command, the first blocker attempts to hook the defender. After the defender defeats the hook block, the next blocker should be instructed to chop block the defender. The running back tries to get the ball outside the defender. The defender defeats both blockers and executes an angle tackle on the ball carrier. The drill should be conducted in both directions and until all defenders have received a sufficient number of repetitions.

Coaching Points:

1. Instruct the defensive end to defeat the blockers one at a time. Don't look beyond the blocker to the next blocker or to the ball carrier.

2. The defensive end must keep his outside leg and arm free at all times.

3. The defensive end should attack upfield and execute an angle tackle on the ball carrier.

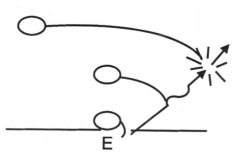

6 CAT AND MOUSE DRILL

Purpose: To teach proper position, footwork and relationship on quarterback when slow playing the option.

Execution: Use the backup quarterback and backup running backs to execute this drill. Align the offensive personnel on a selected line of scrimmage. Position a defensive end in proper alignment. On the cadence, instruct the quarterback to run at the defensive end and read his technique. The running back must work to stay in pitch phase. The defensive end should slow play the quarterback, make him pitch the ball, and pursue inside-out on the running back. The drill should be conducted in both directions and until all defenders have had a sufficient number of repetitions.

Coaching Points:

1. Instruct the defensive end to shuffle, keeping his outside foot back and his hips cocked slightly to the inside.

2. The defensive end must keep at least an arm's distance away from the quarterback. If the quarterback decides to keep the ball and cut up inside, the defensive end must be in position to make the play for little or no gain. If the quarterback pitches the ball, the defensive end must pursue inside- out on the ball carrier. The defensive end must create indecision in the quarterback's mind and buy time to get to the ball.

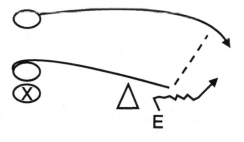

PASS RUSH

The pass defense is only as good as the pass rush. If the defensive front allows the quarterback to sit back in the pocket unmolested, the quarterback will pick the coverage apart. It's imperative that the rush puts pressure on the quarterback. Forcing the quarterback to move his feet, throw the ball early, batting the ball down, hitting the quarterback as he throws or sacking the quarterback are examples of an effective pass rush.

ESSENTIALS OF PASS RUSH TECHNIQUE

Take-off

The most important factor on successful pass rush is the take-off. From the moment of movement, the defender must close the distant between himself and the blocker as quickly as possible, so the blocker has as little time as possible to set up and prepare for the move.

Target

The defender must know prior to the snap where he wants to aim and at what points he wants to take the blocker on. The defender should punch into the offensive lineman, forcing him to retreat from the line of scrimmage as quickly as possible. The defensive linemen should work to get their hands and arms fully extended to gain and maintain separation from the blocker.

Plan

The defensive lineman should always have a plan to execute when he reaches the target point. The plan should be based upon a number of factors:
1. His ability and his best moves
2. What moves have been executed before
3. The blocker's strengths and weaknesses.
4. What physical advantages he may have over the blocker, such as speed, strength and agility.

COUNTER

The defender must always have a counter move ready in case the blocker picks up the initial move. One of the key points is that the defensive linemen must be moving upfield at all times. They should never be allowed to come to a stop, or make lateral or stationary moves. The second effort is the difference between success and failure in pass rush technique.

PASS RUSH LANES

It is imperative that the defenders remain in their pass rush lanes when rushing the quarterback. If a defensive lineman gets out of his lane, it opens a "window" for the quarterback to look downfield and could also lead to losing containment on the quarterback. With a base four-man rush, we teach our two outside ends to rush with contain responsibilities to the shoulder of the quarterback. Our two inside tackles have inside rush responsibilities aiming for the near number of the quarterback. As the quarterback moves out of the pocket, the defenders are taught to keep the same target on the quarterback to help constrict the pocket and keep contain responsibilities.

1 PASS RUSH AGAINST A ONE-MAN SLED

Purpose: To teach defensive linemen proper pass rush techniques.

Equipment: One-man sled.

Execution: Position the defensive linemen in a line directly in front of the one-man sled. Align a stand up dummy representing the quarterback's drop seven yards behind the selected line of scrimmage. The coach or manager gives the movement key with the snap of a ball. On the snap, the defensive lineman explodes into the blocking sled and executes a designated move and then rushes upfield to the quarterback (bag). The drill should be conducted from both sides and until all defensive linemen have had a sufficient number of repetitions.

Coaching Points:

1. Check for proper stance and take-offs. Change up cadence.

2. Check for proper pass rush technique.

3. Make sure the defender stays in his pass rush lane and aims for appropriate target on the quarterback.

Variation: Work the counter moves.

E

2 RAPID FIRE

Purpose: To employ all pass rush techniques in a controlled environment.

Execution: Divide defensive linemen into two groups. Position three defenders in a single file line, three yards apart. The defensive player will face the first of three blockers in a line. On the coach's command, the defender will consecutively engage and execute a pass rush technique on each of the blockers. The drill should be conducted until all defenders have had a sufficient number of repetitions.

Coaching Points:

1. Check for proper form and technique in each of the defender's moves.

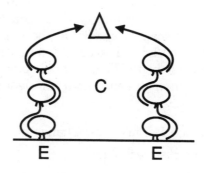

3 INSIDE PASS RUSH

Purpose: To teach the progression of inside pass rush technique.

Execution: Divide defensive linemen into two groups and position them on a selected line of scrimmage. Groups should be paired up, with one player designated as offense and the other as defense. The players face each other in a locked out position. On command, the defender drives the blocker back, breaks down his block, and executes an escape move. The drill should be conducted until all defensive linemen have had a sufficient number of repetitions.

Coaching Points:

1. Check to see that the defender drives the blocker upfield before executing an escape move.
2. Check for proper technique and footwork.

Variations:

- Inside pass rush drill from regular stance and alignment.
- Work counter moves.

4 CONTAIN RUSH

Purpose: To teach proper technique for contain rush.

Execution: Divide the defensive linemen into two groups. Designate one man in each line to represent the offensive blocker. Position a stand up dummy to represent the quarterback's drop. On the cadence, the blocker will set to the inside. The defender explodes out of his stance and executes designated pass rush technique. After defeating the block, the defender must continue to squeeze to the appropriate shoulder of the quarterback. The drill should be conducted until all defensive linemen receive a sufficient number of repetitions.

Coaching Points:

1. Check for proper stance and take-offs.

2. Check for proper pass rush technique.

3. Make sure rusher maintains contain responsibilities.

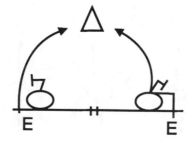

5 PASS RUSH AGAINST A SCRAMBLING QUARTERBACK

Purpose: To teach the defensive linemen to stay in proper relationship to the quarterback as he leaves the pocket.

Execution: Position the first defensive line on a selected line of scrimmage. Align three cones seven yards deep and 10 yards apart from the line of scrimmage. The quarterback will drop back behind a certain cone. The defenders will cross the line of scrimmage and break down in front of the cones. The quarterback will scramble from side to side trying to break contain or split the defenders. The drill should be conducted until all defensive linemen receive a sufficient number of repetitions.

Coaching Points:

1. Use a mobile athlete to play the quarterback position.
2. Make sure defenders move their feet and keep their shoulders square.
3. Make sure defenders stay together and keep their proper relationship to the quarterback.
4. Instruct the quarterback to look for a seam and try to split the defenders.

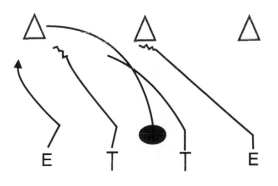

12
LINEBACKER DRILLS

"Make your opponent fear and respect you"

— Knute Rockne

STANCE

The stance of the linebacker is commonly called the "hitting position," a two-point stance with the feet parallel and shoulder width apart. The linebacker's weight should be on the balls of his feet, shoulders over the toes, knees bent, with a slight bend at the waist and the butt down. The hands should be relaxed and dangle above or to the inside of the knees. The stance should allow the linebacker to do a variety of things:

1. See the key.
2. Move forward.
3. Move laterally.
4. Move backward.
5. Turn and run.
6. Step in all directions and never raise the head from the original position.

MOVEMENT

When the ball is snapped and the linebacker reads the run, the linebackers should attack the line of scrimmage. In order to do this, the linebacker must keep his shoulders square and attack downhill. If the linebacker turns and runs, cut back seams develop in the front.

1 SHUFFLE DRILL

Purpose: To teach linebackers to keep their shoulders square and develop feet agility.

Equipment: Five dummies and two cones.

Execution: Linebackers stand in a single file line behind the cone. The coach gives a "set" command and the first linebacker steps up to a good football hitting position. On the next command, "hit," the linebacker shuffles over the bags leading with his right foot. As the linebacker crosses the last dummy, he turns and sprints past the cone. The drill is repeated in the opposite direction and should be conducted until all linebackers have had a sufficient number of repetitions.

Coaching Points:

1. Check to see that linebackers are in the correct stance.
2. Linebackers should be low, with the shoulders square and the head up.
3. Hands should be out front to protect legs.
4. No crossover steps, players should always lead with the inside foot.

Variation: Incorporate a football and toss it back and forth with the linebacker as he shuffles through the bags.

2 ANGLE SHUFFLE DRILL

Purpose: To develop downhill shuffle technique and foot agility.

Equipment: Four dummies.

Execution: Position four dummies one yard apart at a 45-degree angle. The coach gives a "set" command and the first linebacker steps up in a good football hitting position. On the next command, "hit," the linebacker shuffles over the bags leading with his right foot. The drill should be executed in both directions and until all linebackers have had a sufficient number of repetitions.

Coaching Points:

1. Check for proper stance.
2. Make sure linebackers stay low, shoulders square and head up.
3. Emphasize linebackers working down hill and attacking the line of scrimmage.
4. Rotate bags to work lead step with other foot.

Variation: Incorporate a football and toss it back and forth with linebacker as he shuffles through the bags.

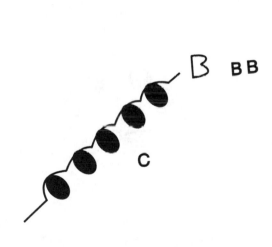

3 LINEBACKER ATTACK DRILL

Purpose: To develop downhill shuffle and foot agility.

Equipment: Four dummies.

Execution: Align two rows of dummies one yard apart at a 45-degree angle. Position linebackers in a single file line between the two rows of dummies. On the coach's command, "set", the first linebacker steps up in a good hitting position. The coach then gives a directional signal and the linebacker attacks downhill. The linebacker should break down in a good hitting position as he crosses the final bag. The drill should be conducted so all linebackers receive a sufficient number of repetitions.

Coaching Points:

1. Check for proper stance.

2. The linebacker should lead with the foot in the direction the coach points. Do not allow crossovers and eliminate false steps.

3. The linebacker should stay low, keeping his shoulders square and head up.

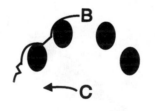

DELIVERING A BLOW

Approach

The linebacker should attack the blocker with his shoulders square while maintaining a good base. The linebacker should never wait for the blocker to come for him; he should attack and be the aggressor. The linebacker should stay low and maintain proper leverage.

Contact

We teach our linebackers to attack blockers with three-point contact. It is imperative that the linebacker keeps his eyes on the blocker so that he can distinguish the type of block. The linebacker should make contact with his eye-level below the blocker's chin. On contact, the linebacker should shoot his hands into the blocker's chest and explode through the blocker by extending his legs. He must stop his momentum by snapping the blocker's head back. As soon as the linebacker stops the blocker's momentum, he should extend his arms and work for separation. When the ball carrier commits, the linebacker should shed the block and get to the football.

1 POPSICLE DRILL

Purpose: To teach linebackers proper fundamentals involved in three-point contact.

Equipment: One-man sled.

Execution: Align linebackers in a single file line in front of the popsicle sled. On the coach's first command, the linebacker steps up in a good stance two yards in front of the sled. On the coach's second command, the linebacker attacks the sled with proper three-point contact. The linebacker should have separation and continue to move his feet until the coach blows the whistle. The linebacker should shed the popsicle, take two steps upfield and break down into a good hitting position. The drill should be conducted until all linebackers have had a sufficient number of repetitions.

Coaching Points:

1. Check for proper stance.

2. The linebacker should attack the sled with three-point contact while maintaining a good base.

3. Emphasize rolling the hips on contact and work for separation.

4. The linebacker should shed the block and break down in a good hitting position.

Variations:

- See also "Six-point explosion" and "Four-point explosion" in the Defensive Line section.
- See also the "Oklahoma Drill" in the Tackling section.

2 FOUR MAN BUTT

Purpose: To teach proper blow delivery technique.

Execution: Align three defenders in a semi-circle with a linebacker in the middle. The coach points to a designated defender to set up and block the linebacker. The linebacker feels which man is coming out to block him and attacks the blocker with a proper blow delivery technique. After all three defenders execute blocks, the drill rotates clockwise. The drill should continue until all personnel have had a sufficient number of repetitions at the linebacker position.

Coaching Points:

1. Check for proper stance.

2. Make sure linebacker attacks with proper blow delivery technique, separates from the blocker, and backs up ready to take on the next man.

3. This is a good drill to set the tempo for practice.

3 ONE-ON-ONE READ DRILL

Purpose: To teach proper reads and reactions to uncovered linemen.

Execution: Place two defenders three yards apart and designate a defender to play the offensive lineman position. Position the lineman in between the two cones and align a linebacker in base alignment. The coach designates the lineman's blocking technique (i.e. base, down block, zone scheme, pull, trap, pass set) On the cadence, the lineman carries out his technique and the linebacker reacts accordingly. The drill should be conducted until all linebackers receive a sufficient number of repetitions.

Coaching Points:

1. Check for proper stance and alignment.
2. Make sure the designated lineman gives proper reads.
3. Check to see that the linebacker reads and reacts accordingly.

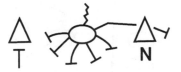

4 TREE OF BLOCKS DRILL

Purpose: To teach the linebackers proper reads and reactions to different blocking schemes.

Execution: Use either the backup offensive linemen or linebackers to play the center, guard, tackle, and fullback positions. Position the backup defensive linemen to represent defensive front alignment. Coach designates blocking scheme and course of fullback. On the cadence, the offensive group carries out its responsibilities and the linebacker reacts accordingly. The drill should be conducted until all linebackers receive a sufficient number of repetitions.

Coaching Points:

1. Check for proper stance and alignment.

2. Make sure the offensive unit carries out correct responsibilities.

3. Check to see that the linebacker reads and reacts accordingly.

Variation: See also the "Iso Drill" in the Running Back Section.

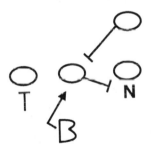

AGAINST A LOW BLOCK

It is imperative that the linebacker concentrate on the blocker. He should "feel" the ball carrier with his peripheral vision, but keep his eyes on the blocker. The linebacker should read the blocker's head, approaching the block in a good football position with the hands ready to deliver a blow. The linebacker should punch the blocker with the palms of his hands through the helmet and shoulder in the direction the helmet is taking. He should then shuffle, stay square to the line of scrimmage and give ground, slightly pressing the blocker's helmet and shoulder pad down and away from his body. The linebacker should keep his hips and legs out of the blocker and pursue to the football.

1 CHOP BLOCK DRILL

Purpose: To teach proper fundamentals in defending the chop block and executing an angle tackle.

Execution: Position three linebackers (chop blockers) on their hands and knees two yards apart at a 45-degree angle. Position a ball carrier five yards behind the third blocker and a cone five yards outside of his position. Align the remaining linebackers in a single file line. On the coach's command, the first linebacker shuffles downhill and defeats the first chop block. He should now square up and wait for the next command. The drill is repeated until the linebacker defeats the third blocker. On the coach's next command, the ball carrier takes off to the cone and the linebacker executes an angle tackle. The drill should be conducted in both directions and until all linebackers have had a sufficient number of repetitions.

Coaching Points:

1. Check for proper stance.
2. The linebacker should always start the drill aligned inside of the chop blocker.
3. Check to see that linebackers are executing proper technique in defending the chop block.
4. Make sure the linebacker executes proper technique on the angle tackle.

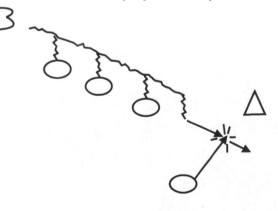

LINEBACKER PASS DROPS

The linebacker's objective in zone coverage is to make the opponent throw the ball short. If the ball is thrown in the intermediate zones, the linebackers must either intercept the ball or force the quarterback to throw the ball high to give the deep secondary an opportunity to break on the ball. If the ball is thrown short, the linebackers should break up on the ball and either force the ball loose with a hit or make the tackle for a short gain. The linebacker's responsibility against a pass is dictated by various coverages. There is, however, a progression in defending the pass in zone coverage.

Read

The linebacker should recognize the pass by reading his initial key. Coach the linebackers to be aware of certain pre-snap reads that may tip off a pass. The opponent's formations, stance, and "down and distance" situation should alert the linebacker of a passing situation.

Drop

The linebacker should begin his movement to his drop point. The drop may or may not be dependent upon a second or third receiver, but he should always feel the nearest threat. The linebacker should either backpedal or open up, depending on where the drop point is in regard to his alignment on the field.

Position

When the quarterback sets up to throw, the linebacker should be squared to the line of scrimmage, with the hips down and eyes focused on the front shoulder of the quarterback. If the quarterback is focused toward the linebacker, he should sit down and be ready to react laterally in either direction. If the quarterback is focused away from the linebacker, he should begin to fade in that direction. The linebacker must see the ball thrown and recognize the various launch points.

Break

When the quarterback's front hand comes off the ball, the linebacker should drive in the direction of the quarterback's focus. As the linebacker breaks, he must recognize whether he can or cannot get to the ball. If he can, he should make the interception. If not, he should be instructed to go through the receiver. Anticipation and reaction are the keys.

1 INTERCEPTION DRILL

Purpose: To develop pass catching skills.

Execution: Align the linebackers in a single file line. On the coach's command, the first linebacker starts off on a backpedal. The coach gives a directional signal and the linebacker breaks off at a 45-degree angle. The linebacker intercepts the football and returns the ball upfield. The drill should be conducted so all linebackers receive a sufficient number of repetitions.

Coaching Points:

1. Check for proper stance.

2. The linebacker should open his hips in the direction of the signal.

3. Instruct the linebacker to catch the football at its highest point and sprint back.

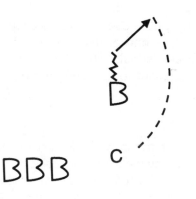

2 ZONE DROP DRILL

Purpose: To teach the linebackers drop points and break on the football.

Execution: The drill begins in the middle of the field. Position three defenders 12 to 15 yards deep. The two outside defenders should be aligned on the hashmark, and the third defender should be aligned in the middle of the field. Position two linebackers in proper stances and alignments. On the snap, the quarterback (or coach) takes a five or seven step drop. The linebackers should take the proper drop, square up and break on the ball. The drill should be conducted from both hashmarks and until all linebackers have had a sufficient number of repetitions.

Coaching Points:

1. Check for proper stances.

2. Check for proper drop technique.

3. Instruct linebackers to square up when the quarterback sets his feet and break on the ball.

4. The linebacker who doesn't intercept the ball should block the intended receiver.

3 ROUTE READING DRILL

Purpose: To teach the linebackers proper route reads and drop point.

Execution: Align one defender 15 yards deep in the middle of the field, another defender 14 yards deep on the hashmark, and a third defender five yards deep over the football. Position a fourth defender in the tight end position. The first linebacker aligns accordingly in a proper stance. The coach designates a route for the tight end to run (flat, cross or vertical). On the cadence, the tight end runs the designated route, and the quarterback takes either a five or seven step drop. The linebacker should look up the tight end and react accordingly. The quarterback should be instructed to throw to either of the two defenders downfield or dump the ball off. The linebacker should square up and get a break on the football. The drill should be conducted from various positions on the field and until all linebackers have had a sufficient number of repetitions.

Coaching Points:

1. Check for proper stance and alignment.

2. Check to see if linebacker is taking the appropriate drop off the tight end's route.

3. The linebacker should be squared up by the time the quarterback sets up.

4. Check for the break on the ball.

Variation: See also "Half line pass" and "Skeleton" in the Group Pass section.

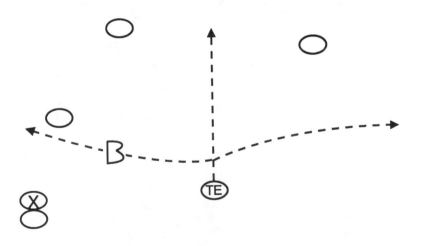

MAN-TO-MAN COVERAGE

In order to change up and blitz an opponent, it is necessary to play man-to-man coverage. In most cases, linebackers are matched up with running backs or tight ends. The linebacker man-to-man progression consists of three phases.

Read

When the ball is snapped, the linebacker must locate his man. His eyes should be focused on the man, not looking back at the ball.

Position

The linebacker should move laterally as he closes on his man. He wants to take away the distance between the two of them as quickly as possible. The linebacker should work for an inside position on the receiver by placing his hands and sternum on his inside number. This will prevent the man from breaking inside.

Close

As the receiver runs his route, the linebacker should work to keep an inside and upfield position on the man. When the man breaks off his route, it is imperative that the linebacker keeps his concentration on him. If the linebacker looks back for the ball, the receiver will create a greater distance between them. The linebacker must remain focused and drive for the upfield shoulder of the receiver.

1   MAN-TO-MAN AGAINST RUNNING BACK AND TIGHT END ROUTES

Purpose: To teach proper man technique for linebackers against running back and tight end routes.

Execution: Divide linebackers into two groups and designate one group as offense and the other as the linebackers. Half of the offensive group will align as the tight end, and the other half will align as the running back. The coach designates the route. On command, the tight end/running back executes the route. The linebacker executes proper man technique against the tight end and running back routes. The drill should be conducted so all linebackers receive a sufficient number of repetitions.

Coaching Points:

1. Check for proper stance.

2. Run one route at a time.

3. Make sure the linebacker keeps inside position on receiver.

4. Don't use a football. Make the linebacker concentrate on the man.

Variation: See also the "Individual Cuts" drill in the Group Pass section.

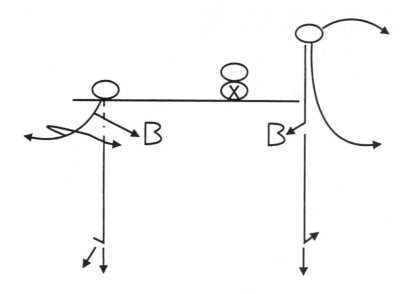

13
SECONDARY DRILLS

"It's not the size of the dog in the fight, it's the size of the fight in the dog."

— author unknown

STANCE

The defensive back's stance should be one which will enable him to backpedal effectively. The feet should be staggered with a heel to toe relationship, no wider than shoulder width apart. The weight should be balanced over both feet to eliminate any false stepping. The defensive back should bend at the waist, bend his knees, keep his tail up, and his shoulders down. The back should be rounded slightly, the head up and the eyes forward on the quarterback. The arms should be relaxed, hanging down from the shoulders.

START

If the defensive back doesn't start his backward run by taking a step back, he'll seriously handicap his ability to cover. If either foot comes forward, he'll lose two steps in coverage (false step). It is a good idea to teach the defensive backs to push off with their inside foot and step back with their outside foot. The defensive back should keep his shoulders low and his center of gravity over the balls of his feet.

BACKPEDAL

A defensive back must learn to stay low when backpedaling. He should remain bent at the waist while keeping his shoulders over his thighs. The arm should swing freely in a normal running fashion. The feet should be slightly less than shoulder width apart. The overall action should be similar to one running forward, except that the mechanics are reversed. The defensive back should actually reach back with each step and pull his body over his feet as he does when running forward.

1 BACKPEDAL DRILL

Purpose: To teach defensive backs proper backpedaling technique.

Execution: Divide the defensive backs into two groups aligned on the sideline. On the coach's command, the defensive backs should backpedal to the hash mark. When the defensive backs reach the hash mark, the coach points a direction for the back to break. After each repetition, the defensive backs must switch lines. The drill continues until all defensive backs have had a sufficient number of repetitions.

Coaching Points:

1. Check for proper stance and starts.

2. Emphasize staying low and sliding fast across the grass. They must not overstride.

3. The weight should be distributed over the balls of the feet.

4. Make sure the defensive back's eyes are focused on the coach.

5. Use the yard lines to make sure the defensive backs are backpedaling in a straight line.

Variation: Incorporate a ball and throw to one of the defensive backs.

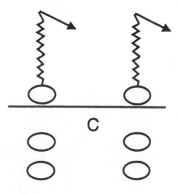

2 WEAVE DRILL

Purpose: To teach defensive backs to keep proper leverage on the receiver while staying in their backpedal.

Execution: Divide the defensive backs into two groups aligned on the sideline. On the coach's command, the defensive backs begin backpedaling straight back. The coach gives hand signals for the direction of the weave. When the backs reach the hashmark, the coach gives a direction for the defensive backs to break. After each repetition, the defensive backs must switch lines. The drill continues until all defensive backs have had a sufficient number of repetitions.

Coaching Points:

1. Check for proper stance and starts.

2. The defensive backs should steer their bodies with their hips and feet.

3. Emphasis should be on not crossing the feet and keeping the shoulders square to the line of scrimmage.

4. Make sure the backs use proper backpedaling techniques.

5. Proper form and mechanics are a must. Teach the drill at half speed and gradually increase.

Variation: Incorporate a ball and throw to one of the defensive backs.

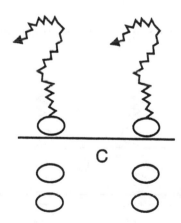

3   QUICK HIPS

Purpose: To increase hip flexibility and balance.

Execution: Divide the defensive backs into two groups aligned on the sideline. On the coach's command, the defensive backs begin backpedaling. The coach will point in a direction. The defensive back must open up and run on the signal. The coach then points in the opposite direction, the defensive back pivots, opens up in that direction, and then sprints down the line. The coach then gives a directional signal for the defensive backs to break. The drill should continue until all defensive backs have had a sufficient number of repetitions.

Coaching Points:

1. Check for proper stance and starts.

2. On the turn signal, emphasis should be on staying low and driving the near elbow to get the hips opened up.

3. Use the yard lines to emphasize staying in a straight line. The players must not drift.

4. Stress proper backpedaling techniques throughout the drill.

Variations:

- Incorporate a ball and throw to one of the defensive backs.
- Using the same set up, have defensive backs open up at 45-degree angles.

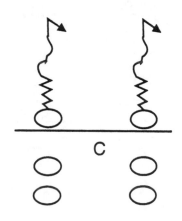

4   ZONE TURN DRILL

Purpose: To teach proper zone turn technique.

Execution: Divide the defensive backs into two groups aligned on the sideline. On the coach's command, the defensive backs begin to backpedal. The coach gives a directional signal; the defensive backs execute proper zone turn technique and sprint to the hash mark. After each repetition, the defensive backs switch lines, working both right and left zone turns. The drill should continue until all defensive backs have had a sufficient number of repetitions.

Coaching Points:

1. Check for proper stance and starts.

2. On the turn signal, the emphasis should be on driving the near elbow to get hips opened up.

3. The defensive back should accelerate through the turn to get out of his backpedal and into his sprint as quickly as possible.

4. The zone turn should be on fluid motion.

5. Use the yard lines to make sure the defensive backs are not drifting.

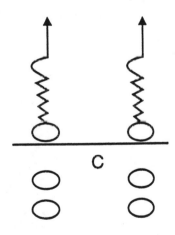

5 CENTERFIELD TURN

Purpose: To teach proper centerfield turn technique.

Execution: Divide the defensive backs into two groups aligned on the sideline. On the coach's command, the defensive backs begin to backpedal. The coach then gives a direction signal for the defensive backs to execute a zone turn. On the coach's next signal, (opposite direction) the defensive backs execute a centerfield turn at 45 degrees. The drill should be conducted with the centerfield turn executed to both the right and left. The drill is executed until all defensive backs have had a sufficient number of repetitions.

Coaching Points:

1. Check for proper stance and starts.

2. Check for proper zone turn techniques.

3. Emphasis should be on getting the head around as quickly as possible to relocate the football and the receiver.

Variation: Incorporate a football and throw to one of the defensive backs.

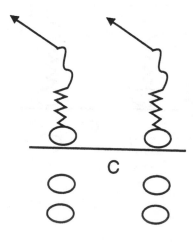

BREAK POINT

It is imperative for defensive backs to have the ability to get out of their backpedal and close on receivers or ball carriers as quickly as possible. Stopping the backward run and making the transition to a forward movement requires proper body position in the pre-break position and proper footwork.

The two key factors in body position are that the defensive back stays low in his backpedal and that the defensive back keeps his feet from getting overextended outside the framework of his body.

The footwork involved in breaking on a ball or ball carrier consists of three steps:

1. Plant step

2. Directional step

3. Cross-over step

The plant step is used to stop the backward momentum and should be with the foot opposite the direction intended to break. The second directional step should be placed in front of the plant step and pointing in the desired direction. It is at this point that a defensive back will often round his break off. The third cross-over step serves as the acceleration step and enables the defensive back to close the ground on the ball or ball carrier.

1 W-DRILL

Purpose: To teach the defensive backs proper techniques when breaking on the receiver or on the ball.

Execution: Divide defensive backs into two groups and align them five yards apart, standing on the side line. On the coach's command, the two defensive backs begin backpedaling at a 45-degree angle. When the defensive backs reach the next yard line, they should execute proper break technique, driving up at a 45-degree angle. The drill continues from one sideline to the other. When all the defensive backs reach the far sideline, repeat the drill coming back up the field to work the break technique in opposite direction.

Coaching Points:

1. Check for proper stance and starts.
2. Check for proper backpedaling techniques.
3. When defensive backs are breaking to their left, their plant step should be with their right foot and vice-versa.
4. Make sure defensive backs are backpedaling and breaking in straight lines.
5. The drill should be taught at half speed and gradually increased.

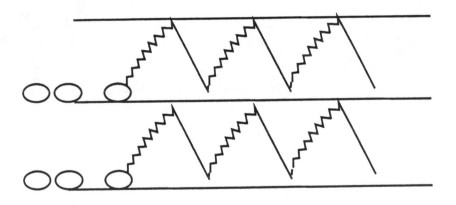

2 BACKPEDAL AND DRIVE

Purpose: To teach the defensive backs proper techniques when breaking on the receiver or on the ball.

Execution: Divide the defensive backs into two groups aligned on the sideline. On the coach's command, the defensive backs begin backpedaling. The coach then gives a visual hand signal to the left or right to determine the direction to plant and drive 45-degrees. The defensive backs should change lines after each repetition. The drill should continue until all defensive backs have had a sufficient number of repetitions.

Coaching Points:

1. Check for proper stance and starts.
2. Check for proper backpedaling techniques.
3. Make sure defensive backs execute proper break technique.
4. Emphasis should be on changing direction as quickly as possible.
5. Do not round breaks.

Variation: Incorporate a football and throw to one of the defensive backs.

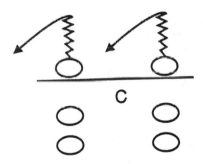

3 POST COMEBACK

Purpose: To teach the defensive backs proper break techniques when they are not in a backpedal.

Execution: Divide the defensive backs into two groups and align them on the sideline. On the coach's command, the defensive backs begin backpedaling. The coach then gives a hand signal left or right to determine the direction in which the player should open up and run at 45-degrees. On the coach's next command, the defensive backs should plant and sprint back to the original line of scrimmage. The drill continues until all defensive backs have had a sufficient number of repetitions.

Coaching Points:

1. Check for proper stance and starts.

2. Check for proper backpedaling technique and for post turn execution.

3. The defensive back should plant off his upfield foot, lower his center of gravity, get his directional step down as quickly as possible, cross over and accelerate back to the original line of scrimmage.

4. The emphasis should be on not rounding the break.

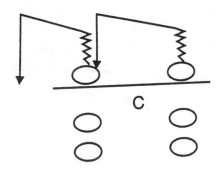

4 ZONE TURN-OUT

Purpose: To teach defensive backs to break on the out-cut after executing a zone turn.

Execution: Align the defensive backs on top of the numbers in a single file line. The coach assumes the position of the quarterback. On the coach's command, the first defensive back begins backpedaling. As the coach opens his shoulders, the defensive back should execute a zone turn. When the coach begins his throwing motion, the defensive back should plant and drive to the out-cut. The drill should be conducted in both directions and until all defensive backs have had a sufficient number of repetitions.

Coaching Points:

1. Check for proper stance, start and backpedaling technique.
2. Make sure the defensive back executes proper zone turn technique.
3. As the defensive back drives on the out-cut, he should plant off his upfield foot, rotate his hips, get his second step down as quickly a possible, and accelerate on the out-cut.

Variation:

- Incorporate a ball and throw the out-cut.
- Have the defensive back read the coach's shoulders. The coach should throw the fade route or out-cut.

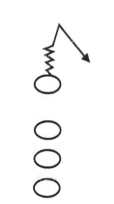

BALL DRILLS

Too often a defensive back is said to either have good hands or bad hands and not much is done to help players who lack natural catching ability. The coach should teach the same ball receiving technique to the defensive backs as they do to their receivers. The defensive backs must concentrate on the football and watch it all the way into their hands. In addition to incorporating footballs in most backpedaling drills, break drills and tackling drills, it is important to incorporate them in interception drills as well. This enables the defensive back to work on catching the football.

1 LINE BALL DRILL

Purpose: To teach the defensive backs proper ball receiving and intercepting techniques.

Execution: The defensive backs align in a single file line standing on the sideline. On the coach's cadence, the first man in line runs the designated drill. When the coach puts the ball in a passing position, the defenders yell "pass." As the ball is released from the coach's hand, the defenders yell "ball" and as the ball is intercepted, the defenders yell "oskie." After each interception, the defender sprints the ball back to the coach and returns to the end of the line.

Coaching Points:

1. First repetition – high balls. Second repetition – low balls

2. Emphasis on catching the ball without slowing down – "Come back for the ball."

3. The thumbs and index fingers should be placed together when catching a high ball. The pinkies and palms should be placed together while bending at the waist when catching a low ball.

4. Coach proper receiving techniques.

2 LINE BALL DRILL PROGRESSION
– BREAK AT 45-DEGREES

Coaching Points:

1. The defender will break at 45-degrees upfield as the coach's shoulders open.

2. Make sure that the defender uses proper receiving techniques.

3. First repetition – high ball. Second repetition – low ball. Third repetition – ball thrown behind defender.

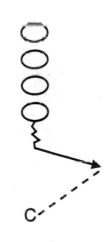

3 LINE BALL DRILL PROGRESSION – TIP DRILL

Coaching Points:

1. The first two men in line take off on coach's command.

2. The first man tips ball up in the air, while the second defender intercepts the ball.

3. Drill teaches players to concentrate on the ball.

4 LINE BALL DRILL PROGRESSION – DUCK DRILL

Coaching Points:

1. The first two men take off on coach's command.
2. The coach throws the football at the first defender's shoulders.
3. As the ball nears the first defender, he should be instructed to duck.
4. The trailing defender should concentrate on the ball all the way into his hands.

5 DEFENSIVE BACK FADE DRILL

Purpose: To teach defensive backs to play the long ball.

Execution: Align the defensive backs at the top of the numbers on a selected line of scrimmage. On command, the first defensive back begins backpedaling. When the coach opens his shoulders, the defensive back should make a zone turn and sprint down the numbers. The coach throws the long ball and the defensive back intercepts it and brings it up the near sideline. The drill should be conducted in both directions and until all defensive backs have had a sufficient number of repetitions.

Coaching Points:

1. Check for proper stance, starts and backpedaling technique.

2. Make sure the defensive back executes proper zone turn technique.

3. Instruct the defensive back to intercept the ball at it's highest point.

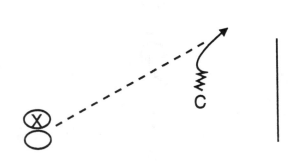

6 ALL GO DRILL

Purpose: To teach defensive backs to play the long ball against two wide receivers in their zone.

Execution: Divide the defensive backs into two groups. Position one group as receivers on the hash marks. Position the second group in the middle of the field representing the defensive backs. The first defensive back will align approximately 10 to 12 yards from the line of scrimmage directly in the middle of the field. On the coach's command, the two wide receivers will sprint down the hash marks as the defensive back begins backpedaling. The coach throws the long ball to either receiver. The defensive back breaks on the throwing action and intercepts the ball. After each repetition, the defensive backs should rotate lines. The drill continues until all defensive backs have had a sufficient number of repetitions.

Coaching Points:

1. Check for proper stance, starts and backpedaling technique.

2. Make sure the defensive back gets a good break on the ball and drives to the interception point

3. Instruct the defensive backs to intercept the ball at the highest point.

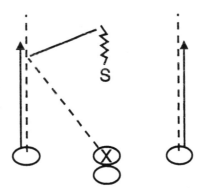

7 BREAK IN FRONT DRILL

Purpose: To teach defensive backs to drive to the interception point and make the interception.

Execution: Align the defensive backs on a selected line of scrimmage in a single file line. Position a defensive back approximately 10 yards deep and four yards outside the line representing the receiver. On the coach's command, the first defensive back begins backpedaling straight back. As the coach opens his shoulders to the receiver, the defensive back should break to the interception point. If the coach throws the ball, the defensive back should intercept the football. If the coach pump fakes, the defensive back should begin his backpedal and break on the out-cut when given the appropriate signal. The drill should be conducted in both directions and until all defensive backs have had a sufficient number of repetitions.

Coaching Points:

1. Check for proper stance, starts and backpedaling technique.

2. Check for proper break technique. Instruct the defensive backs not to round off their breaks.

3. Check for proper ball receiving techniques.

BLOCK PROTECTION

There are basically four types of blocks with which a defensive back must deal: stalk, cut, kickout, and crack. The defensive back must believe that, when he is using the proper technique, a receiver cannot block him. The defensive back must attack the blocker and play through him in protecting his area. This does not mean he should run over the blocker, but that his initial contact should allow him to take the blocker on with proper leverage, rather that running around the block. His goals should be to attack, get separation from the blocker, and react to the ball carrier.

Eyes

When the defensive back recognizes the run and begins to get in his support pattern, it is imperative that his eyes go directly to the intended blocker. The defensive back must see the type of block he will be facing before he can defend it and make the play on the ball carrier.

Punch

The defensive back should attack the blocker by delivering a blow with the heels of the hand. The defensive back should work for inside hand position and lock his arms out. As the defensive back works for separation, he should drive the blocker back on his heels and into the path of the ball carrier.

Whip

After the defensive back has control over the blocker, he should shed him in the opposite direction. The defensive back should use his hands to turn the blockers shoulders, work to get him off balance, and attempt to get beyond him. It is important that the defensive back does not lose sight of the ball carrier or lose leverage when beating a blocker to a side.

Replace

The defensive back should use a rip or swim move to get past the blocker. The defensive back must get his hips and shoulders beyond the blocker and place himself in an unblockable position.

- For block protection drills, see the "Stalk Block" drill in the Wide Receiver Section.
- For man coverage/zone coverage drills, see the "Individual Cuts", "Half Line" and "Skeleton" drills in Chapter 12.

"I don't say these things because I believe in the brute nature of man or that men must be brutalized to be combative. I believe in God, and I believe in human decency. I firmly believe that any man's finest hour – his greatest fulfillment to all he holds dear – is that moment when he has worked his heart out in a good cause and lies exhausted on the field of battle – victorious."

—Vince Lombardi

ABOUT THE AUTHOR

Doug Mallory, son of Hoosier head coach Bill Mallory, is in his first year as Indiana's defensive backfield coach. Mallory played high school football at DeKalb (Ill.) High and then played four years at strong safety at Michigan, where he played in four major bowl games and was co-captain in 1987, when he was 2nd team All Big Ten pick and an honorable mention All-America selection. He is a 1988 graduate of Michigan with a degree in sports management and communications.

Doug served as a graduate assistant coach at Indiana in 1988 before moving to the United States Military Academy as assistant coach in 1989. He moved to Western Kentucky under Jack Harbaugh in 1990 and served four years as defensive back coach, the last two seasons as defensive coordinator. Under Doug's direction, Western's defense ranked 18th nationally in 1993. Mallory and his wife, Lisa, are the parents of a young daughter, Emily.

Get into the game!

Masters Press has a complete line of books on
football and other sports to help coaches
and participants alike "master their game."

All of our books are available at better bookstores
or by calling Masters Press at 1-800-722-2677, or
317-298-5706. Catalogs available upon request.

Our football books include the following:

Conditioning for Football

By Tom Zupancic

Designed to help coaches and players at all levels develop a
conditioning program that improves performance and safety. Includes
strength training principles, aerobic and anaerobic conditioning,
program design and motivation. A unique guide by the strength coach
of the Indianapolis Colts.

$12.95 • paper • 160 pages • b/w photos
ISBN: 0-940279-77-0

Football Crosswords

By Dale Ratermann

A collection of crosswords on each of the 28 National Football League
teams. Each chapter is devoted to a specific team and features a history
of the franchise, relevant statistics, and a crossword puzzle. Fun for all
ages!

$12.95 • paper • 192 pages • photos, puzzles and graphs
ISBN 0-940279-74-6

Coaching Football

By Tom Flores & Bob O'Connor

The most complete guide to the sport of football available! Flores and O'Connor trace the development of the game from the past to the present to the future, and include the latest innovative plays. Informative and inviting, this book is a necessity for coaches who are series about improving their abilities on and off the field.

$14.95 • paper • 192 pages • b/w photos & diagrams

ISBN 0-940279-71-X

Youth League Football

By Tom Flores & Bob O'Connor

Includes drills and coaching suggestions for all positions on the field, along with equipment information and hints for keeping the emphasis on "play" rather than "work." A complete primer!

$12.95 • paper • 192 pages • b/w photos

ISBN 0-940279-69-X

Super Bowl Chronicles

By Jerry Green

The compelling story of that unique American phenomenon, the Super Bowl. Jerry Green, one of only 13 journalists to have covered the first 25 Super Bowls, tells of the unique characters and little-known facts he discovered along the way.

$19.95 • cloth • 192 pages • photo insert

ISBN 0-940279-32-0